The Reformation: A Very Short Introduction

VERY SHORT INTRODUCTIONS are for anyone wanting a stimulating and accessible way into a new subject. They are written by experts, and have been translated into more than 45 different languages.

The series began in 1995, and now covers a wide variety of topics in every discipline. The VSI library now contains over 500 volumes—a Very Short Introduction to everything from Psychology and Philosophy of Science to American History and Relativity—and continues to grow in every subject area.

Titles in the series include the following:

Peter Marshall

THE REFORMATION

A Very Short Introduction

OXFORD
UNIVERSITY PRESS

OXFORD
UNIVERSITY PRESS

Great Clarendon Street, Oxford OX2 6DP

Oxford University Press is a department of the University of Oxford.
It furthers the University's objective of excellence in research, scholarship,
and education by publishing worldwide in

Oxford New York

Auckland Cape Town Dar es Salaam Hong Kong Karachi
Kuala Lumpur Madrid Melbourne Mexico City Nairobi
New Delhi Shanghai Taipei Toronto

With offices in

Argentina Austria Brazil Chile Czech Republic France Greece
Guatemala Hungary Italy Japan Poland Portugal Singapore
South Korea Switzerland Thailand Turkey Ukraine Vietnam

Oxford is a registered trade mark of Oxford University Press
in the UK and in certain other countries

Published in the United States
by Oxford University Press Inc., New York

British Library Cataloguing in Publication Data

Data available

Library of Congress Cataloging in Publication Data

Data available

Typeset by SPI Publisher Services, Pondicherry, India
Printed in Great Britain by
Ashford Colour Press Ltd, Gosport, Hampshire

ISBN 978-0-19-923131-7

In memory of Trevor Johnson (1961–2007)

Contents

List of illustrations

Introduction

The Reformation created modern Europe, and left an indelible mark on the history of the world. But what was the Reformation, and was it a force for progress, liberty, and modernity, or for conflict, division, and repression? Is it history's premier example of religion's ability to inspire selfless idealism and beneficent social change, or a cautionary tale of fanaticism and intolerance in the name of faith? Was it actually about religion at all, or should we see it as the historical instance par excellence of spiritual motivations being cynically invoked to legitimate economic and political changes?

Scholars used to know the answers to these questions, though different scholars knew quite different answers, the Reformation having been as divisive for subsequent historians as it was for those who lived through it. This is because it has always seemed a foundational moment, raising questions of origins and parentage, the culturally and politically contentious issues of who we are and where we come from. Millions of Protestants across the world still look to events in the 16th century as inspiration, as the beginning of their story. It is a story of spiritual liberation, of people casting aside the shackles of theological and moral servitude. The movement initiated by the renegade German friar Martin Luther brought an end to corrupt and oppressive rule by the clergy of an institutional Church, a Church that had maintained its power by imposing superstitious and psychologically burdensome beliefs on ordinary (lay) worshippers. It was also a return to the pure sources of Christianity, after centuries in which the stream was polluted by the dripping pipe of man-made traditions. The bible, the Word of God, was restored to its rightful place as the rule and arbiter of Christian life. In vernacular translations of scripture, lay readers met the person of Jesus Christ, bypassing the clerical mediators who, like officious secretaries, had kept medieval petitioners from direct contact with the boss.

There is a related version of this story, allowing secular liberals to claim the Reformation as part of their heritage too. Luther's protest was a first strike against authoritarianism in many areas of social and intellectual life, a hammer blow against the kind of religion that 'tells you what to think'. Modern individualism has its origins in the unfettered bible-reading the Reformation encouraged; modern capitalism in the industriousness and initiative of Protestant merchants; and modern science in the refusal of deference to ancient authorities. New and potentially liberalizing forms of political organization emerged from the revolt against Rome. The 'problem' with contemporary Islam, newspaper pundits often solemnly assure us, is that it can't produce an Enlightenment, having never had a Reformation. Less fashionable now, though still sometimes touted, is a Marxist view that the Reformation was an example of an 'early bourgeois revolution' to overthrow feudal aristocracy – a vital historical precondition for the later revolution of the proletariat.

There are alternative versions. The 1520 papal bull condemning Luther likened him to a wild boar crashing around in the vineyard of the Lord, and that is how he, and the movement he unleashed, have seemed to many Catholics over the centuries. The Victorian Jesuit poet Gerard Manley Hopkins echoed the papal condemnation in his masterpiece *The Wreck of the Deutschland*, where Luther appears as the 'beast of the waste wood'. Wherever the Reformation triumphed, it ruthlessly destroyed a priceless artistic and cultural inheritance. It also brought down precious structures of community. No longer sustained by a communal, interconnected world of guilds, brotherhoods, and collective rituals, the individual now stood alone as an adherent of the Church and a subject of the state. There are secular variants of this story too. Was the Protestants' insistence on the plain, unvarnished truth of scripture, and on the literal meaning of its text, not the foundation stone of modern fundamentalism and illiberalism? Some modern feminists, in unholy alliance with regretful Catholics, have suspected the Reformation of being bad news for women, reinforcing patriarchal authority in the home, and closing off the career path represented by convents. Meanwhile, modern Christian ecumenists suggest that the whole thing may have been an unfortunate mistake, that Luther and his opponents were really saying the same thing in the course of their ferocious debates about salvation.

These are all myths, which is not to say they are completely untrue. Myths are not lies, but symbolically powerful articulations of sensed realities. It is probably safer to believe that all the myths about the Reformation are true, rather than that none of them are. The goal of producing a totally unmythologized account of the Reformation may be an unachievable, or even an undesirable, one. Nonetheless, this little book – drawing on the best, not always impartial, modern scholarship – will attempt to explain what sort of phenomenon the Reformation was, to assess its impact across religious, political, social, and cultural areas of life, and the character of its legacy to the modern world.

First off, a pretty basic question: was there actually such a thing as 'the Reformation', an expression nobody used in our commonly accepted sense until long after the events it was meant to describe? The call for 'reform' within Christianity is about as old as the religion itself, and in every age there have been urgent attempts to bring it about. Historians have identified a '10th-century reformation' in the English Church, associated with the renewal of Benedictine monasticism, as well as a 12th-century reformation, directed by the papacy, that succeeded in imposing clerical celibacy across the Christian West. The 'Great Schism' of the later 14th century, which produced two (and at one point three) rival claimants to the papal throne, produced an intense desire for *reformatio* in the following century. Reformation in the 15th century had both an official and an unofficial face. Leading churchmen sought to end the crisis of leadership and prevent the scandal of disunity by regularizing the government of the Church through General Councils. Such august bodies met at Pisa (1409), at Constance (1414–18), at Pavia and Siena (1423–4), and at Basle and other sites (1431–49). This 'conciliar' approach to reform died out once the papacy was again strong enough to impose its authority. But in the meantime still more far-reaching reform movements had been set in motion. In England, the theologian John Wyclif (d. 1384) formulated an astonishingly radical critique of the Church of his day, substituting the supreme authority of scripture for that of the pope, and arguing that clergymen should exercise no worldly authority. Wyclif's followers were driven out of the universities, but managed to lay the foundations for an underground heretical movement (the 'Lollards') in the country at large. At the other end of Europe, in the kingdom of Bohemia, another radical priest, Jan Hus, inspired a national revolt against foreign overlordship and Roman jurisdiction. The Hussites also demanded that lay people should receive wine, as well as bread, in the communion at mass. The aims and priorities of reform movements were not always compatible – Hus was burned as a heretic by the Council of Constance – but collectively they give the lie to any suggestion that torpor and complacency were the hallmarks of European religious life in the century before Martin Luther. In the light of so many previous attempts at reformation, why does the one associated with Luther deserve the definite article and the capital letter?

There are strong arguments for saying it shouldn't. Older textbooks on the Reformation typically began the story with Luther's protest in 1517 and wrapped it up not much more than a decade after his death in 1546. The Reformation seemed a fundamentally German event (though there were important reverberations in off-stage places, like England), and it had a neat and clean narrative shape: causes and progression of Luther's break with the Roman Church, and subsequent establishment, against the wishes of the Catholic German emperor, of Protestant state churches. The Reformation was Protestant, it was political, and (given the disordered state of the pre-Reformation Catholic Church) it was predictable.

Neither the chronology nor the geography of this Reformation seems convincing any more. And the assumption that the Reformation was 'inevitable' looks, at the very least, debatable, in the light of new research emphasizing the flexibility and spiritual vigour of late medieval Catholicism. Most significantly, there is now a widespread acceptance that what once seemed the alpha and omega of 16th-century Reformation – the Lutheran movement in Germany – was only one part of a much greater whole. Reformation is giving way to plural reformations: multiple theological and political movements with their own directions and agendas. There were distinct national, regional, and local reformations, not all Lutheran, and not all successful. Dogging the steps of Lutheranism was an ambitious rival brand of Protestant Christianity, often called in theological short-hand 'Calvinism', though 'Reformed' Protestantism is the more correct label. It is sometimes also referred to as the 'Second Reformation', though many places in Europe experienced it as the first alternative to the old faith of Catholicism. Not all the religious experimenters of the age followed the lead of Luther, Calvin, or other 'magisterial' reformers, who taught from a position of authority and allied themselves with secular magistrates. There was also a disparate, bottom-up 'Radical Reformation' of groups and individuals who imagined an entirely different social order, and dared to rethink

Introduction

some basic premises of Christianity that magisterial reformers still took for granted. One of the most important reformations took place within not outside of the Catholic Church, or, as we can begin to call it after serious rivals emerged, the Roman Catholic Church. It has long been recognized that Rome rallied its forces and reordered its ranks in the face of Luther's and Calvin's challenges. In a formula popularized by German Protestant historians of the 19th century, this was dubbed the 'Counter-Reformation', a negative and essentially reactive response. Earlier histories of the Reformation (and a surprising number of current ones) either omit this view from the Tiber or squeeze it into an appendant chapter at the back of the volume. Yet what is increasingly coming to be known as 'The Catholic Reformation' or 'Catholic Renewal' was much more than retrenchment in the face of the enemy. New spiritual and reforming energies within Catholicism predated the Protestant revolt; some were diverted into it, but others not. Catholic reform was naturally shaped by an ongoing confrontation with Protestantism, just as Protestantism defined itself throughout its history in relation to a Catholic, or 'papist', other. It makes little sense to consider the Catholic and Protestant Reformations separately from each other, and their contrasting, and sometimes converging, trajectories are treated side-by-side in this book.

The doctrinal teachings of Protestant and Catholic reformers were inimical and anathema to one another. But their broader aims and aspirations could at times look remarkably similar. Both hoped to create a more spiritual Church, and a more godly, disciplined, and ordered society. And both confronted similar obstacles, in the ignorance, apathy, or sheer bloody-mindedness of local communities who might see little reason to change their ways at the behest of high-minded idealists. Perhaps the most significant change in the study of the Reformation over the past few decades has been the realization that the subject encompasses more than changes in theology and the consolidation of new church structures. Or, to put it another way, church history is too important to leave to the church historians. An expansive 'social history' of the Reformation now grapples with questions of both cause and consequence in relation to the experiences and expectations of ordinary folk. Asking why lay people rallied to the Reformation, abandoning traditional and inherited beliefs, is to open a crucial historical window on their deepest priorities and concerns. Unsurprisingly, investigators have found that these concerns were not identical to those of educated reformers. Common folk in 1520s Germany selected and adapted aspects of the reforming programme that spoke to their needs, demonstrating in the process a capacity for 'agency' which an older tradition of scholarship was not always prepared to allow them. The Reformations affected everyone's eternal destiny – the rules for getting to heaven were revised, refined, or reinforced, and people were expected to know what they were. But they also impacted on virtually all aspects of existence in the meantime, from the political structures under which people lived to the small rituals of everyday life. The artistic and cultural landscape of Europe was reconfigured, as was the intimate environment of marriage, the family, and gender relations. One result of this broadening vision of the Reformation's impact is that a quick sprint from the indulgences controversy of 1517 to the closing of the Council of Trent in 1563 is hardly an adequate frame for making sense of the phenomenon. The forces which the Reformation set in motion were working themselves out for decades, even centuries. No two historians' reformations will be exactly the same length, but my perception is that *circa* 1700 is an appropriate point to pause and take stock.

A long Reformation is by necessity a wide one. The stone may have dropped in Luther's Germany but its ripples were felt much further afield. The Reformation was not quite ubiquitous in the Christian world. Half a millennium earlier, Christian Europe had divided along the fault-line between the Eastern and Western halves of the old Roman Empire. Western 'Latin' or Catholic Christendom acknowledged the authority of the pope; the Eastern or 'Orthodox' churches sought leadership from a variety of patriarchs, the

Introduction

pre-eminent of whom was based in Constantinople, a city falling under the sway of Muslim Turks in 1453. The Reformation was an episode within Latin Christianity; the Orthodox were present as neighbours, and occasional objects of conflict and conversion, rather than as full participants. Nonetheless, the Reformation was a far from narrowly West European event. Since the Iron Curtain came down, and the archives of former Eastern bloc countries have opened up, the extent of religious ferment in Hungary, Bohemia, the Baltic states, and Poland has become clearer. It was by no means a certainty in the 16th century that the latter would end up a citadel of Catholicism. And at almost exactly the same time that the Catholic Reformation was getting its act together in Poland, the foundations for another 21st-century bastion of Roman Catholicism were being laid – in the Philippines. The two centuries of Reformation ferment in Europe saw the first significant European expansion beyond Europe. The connection was partly fortuitous, partly not. The discovery of a 'New World' in the Americas, and the intensification of European contacts with the ancient civilizations of Asia, offered undreamt-of opportunities for evangelization. At the very moment its unity was cracking in its European heartlands, Christianity was able to become a truly world religion for the first time in its history. Conflict in Europe drove that process forward, and in due course its religious divisions were exported globally, with profound consequences for the modern world.

All of this serves to make the point that, contrary to the way it is sometimes taught in schools and universities, the Reformation was much more than an event in 'religious' history. Yet it should not become an exercise in the historical ordering of carts and horses. Traditional ecclesiastical historians insist on the primacy of ideas, the real transformative power exercised by new theologies and ways of seeing the world. By contrast, Marxists, as well as subscribers to trendy sociological and literary theories, instinctively want to 'deconstruct', to discern the 'real' political, class-based or economic motivations behind assertions of religious principle or forms of ritual action. The truth is that any approach which begins with a rigid – and fundamentally modern – distinction between the religious and the secular is unlikely to get us very far. For most people in the 16th and 17th centuries, daily life was heavily sacralized and religion was thoroughly secularized – it is extremely difficult, if not impossible, to strain off 'religion' from separate notions of 'social', 'political', or 'economic' behaviour and motivation. Indeed, it is the interaction between all these categories that makes the Reformation a crucial transformative moment in history.

But – to return to an earlier niggle – if Reformation was multiple interlocking reformations, and the sum of political, social, and religious interactions in Europe and the wider world over the course of two centuries, does the concept of 'The Reformation' really stand up? Has the label simply become a cover-all blanket for a convenient era of history, an alternative to that still woollier historical coverlet, 'early modern'? This book stands by the usefulness of the term, for a simple but crucial reason. 'The Reformation' designates both the period and the process through which a key principle established itself at the heart of European culture: the formation of identity by means of division and conflict. During this era, markers of religious difference sprang up across innumerable aspects of life. For the moment, one example, though an important one, will suffice. In 1582, Pope Gregory XIII drew on the latest scientific advice to decree a reform of the ancient Julian Calendar, which had made the year slightly too long. Catholic Europe quickly adopted the 'Gregorian' Calendar, but Protestant states were deeply suspicious, most only abandoning the Julian reckoning around 1700, and Britain and Sweden holding out till the 1750s. The Reformation had politicized time itself.

Spain, Germany was politically fragmented – a patchwork of petty princedoms, ecclesiastical territories, and self-governing cities, under the nominal suzerainty of the grandly named Holy Roman Emperor. The office was elective, the emperor chosen by seven territorial 'Electors' (including three archbishops). At the time of Luther's entry into the monastery the throne was occupied by the Habsburg dynasty, in the person of Maximilian I. Imperial business was conducted at meetings of the *Reichstag*, or 'diets' of the imperial estates, at which electors, princes, and towns were all represented, and took the opportunity to formulate their grievances, often about the need for reform in the Church.

Germans compensated for political weakness with a passionate cultural and linguistic nationalism. The international scholarly movement for the revival of ancient learning known as humanism (not to be confused with modern secular humanism) had a German limb, which found in the writings of the Roman historian Tacitus descriptions of a free and vigorous Germanic people, underlining a contemporary sense of subjugation. The nasty side of German nationalism was an intense Italo-phobia. The far side of the Alps was a source of moral and cultural corruption – and, with one brief exception, all 15th- and 16th-century popes were Italians. There was a political context for this prejudice; Germany was the one important part of Western Europe outside Italy itself where the papal aspiration to direct 'monarchical' government of the Church still had some real purchase. The kings of France, Spain, and England were dutiful sons of Rome. But in a quiet way they had been nationalizing the Church in their territories, securing the right to nominate bishops, for example, and using that power to reward loyal servants. The vacuum of centralized control in Germany meant that popes retained greater power to appoint to ecclesiastical offices, and, via the prince-bishops, to extract taxation from the populace – always a fertile source of bitterness. Anticlericalism – an antipathy to the political power of the clergy – does not equate to rejection of Church teachings. All the evidence suggests that early 16th-century Germany was a pious and orthodox Catholic society. But national and anticlerical resentments abounded, and they found their voice in Luther.

The Luther affair

On 31 October 1517, Luther nailed a long list of points for disputation – Ninety-Five Theses – to the door of the church near the castle in the Saxon capital of Wittenberg. It is a moment that has reverberated in history, the day on which the Protestant Reformation was born and the Middle Ages suddenly dropped dead. The reality is more prosaic. Some scholars have denied that the Theses were ever posted at all. It seems likely that they were, but this was hardly a world-shattering act. Luther was now a professor at the recently founded University of Wittenberg, and the conventional method of initiating academic debate within the theology faculty was to post theses in advance. Because of its handy location, the door of the Castle Church served as the university's bulletin board, and Luther's gesture has been seen as no more dramatic than pinning up a lecture list in a modern college. The Theses themselves were not particularly revolutionary: they did not reject the authority of the pope, or call for the founding of a new church, and they addressed a fairly minor and obscure point of theology. There was in 1517 no blueprint to reform the Church, no foreseeable outcome. Political circumstances, combined with Luther's stubbornness and eventual willingness to think the unthinkable, allowed it all to get out of hand.

The original issue was indulgences. These were an outgrowth of the Church's teaching on sin and penance. Confession to a priest guaranteed forgiveness from God, but the legal-minded thinking of the Middle Ages maintained this still left a 'debt' to be paid for sin. Some of this could be worked off in this life through performance of penances. The rest would be extracted in purgatory – a place in the afterlife where the souls of all but the truly wicked and the excessively saintly would suffer for a while before being admitted,

AETHERNA IPSE SVAE MENTIS SIMVLACHRA LVTHERVS
EXPRIMIT·AT VVLTVS CERA LVCAE OCCIDVOS

·M·D·X·X·

1. Lucas Cranach's 1520 portrait of Martin Luther depicts him as
still very much the Catholic friar

debt-free and purified, into heaven. Indulgences were a certificate remitting some of the punishment due in purgatory in exchange for performance of a good work (they were originally developed as an inducement for people to go on crusade) or giving money to a good cause. Popes argued that, as heads of the Church on earth, they could draw on the 'surplus' good deeds of the saints to underwrite indulgences. The system had a coherent underlying logic, but it was open to abuse, and had been criticized by some thinkers, especially humanists, long before Luther. The papal indulgence issued in 1515 looked particularly dodgy from the viewpoint of moralists and reformers. It was designed to raise money for a prestige project, the building of the new Renaissance Basilica of St Peter in Rome. Its sale in Germany was arranged by one of the worst of the worldly prince-bishops, Albrecht of Brandenburg, who was to keep a share of the proceeds to pay back the bankers who had financed his purchase of the archbishopric of Mainz. Fronting the campaign was a Dominican friar, Johan Tetzel, who went about his business in an effective but crude and materialistic way, employing the advertising jingle, 'as soon as the coin in the coffer rings, a soul from purgatory to heaven springs'. Luther was appalled by Tetzel's methods, and by a popular response which seemed to show no understanding of the need for true repentance. There was also no love lost between the Dominicans and the Augustinians. When Pope Leo X first heard of the controversy, he dismissed it lightly as 'a quarrel among friars'.

Luther meanwhile was edging towards a momentous conclusion – if the Church and pope could or would not reform an evident abuse like indulgences, then something must be wrong with the entire structure of authority and theology. For some years Luther had been nurturing doubts about the elaborate ritual mechanisms for acquiring 'merit' in the eyes of God, and coming to the view that faith alone was sufficient for salvation. Luther's 'radicalization' came into full view in the course of a 1519 debate staged in Leipzig, against a clever orthodox opponent, Johan Eck. Earlier, Luther had conventionally appealed against the pope to the authority of a general council. But by comparing Luther to Jan Hus, Eck manoeuvred him into declaring that the Czech heretic had been unjustly condemned by the Council of Constance, and that councils, like popes, could err in matters of faith. This left only the scripture as an infallible source of religious authority. After Leipzig, there was no going back. Luther was excommunicated by Leo X in 1520, and responded, characteristically, by publicly burning the papal bull of excommunication in Wittenberg. He also published a series of pamphlets castigating the 'Babylonian captivity' of the Church, rejecting the necessity of obedience to the Church's canon law, reducing the number of sacraments from seven to three, and calling on the emperor and German nobility to step in and reform the Church.

Why did what is sometimes seen as an authoritarian Church not crush Luther sooner, before he could do so much damage? The answer is mired in German and international politics. In January 1519, Emperor Maximilian died. The obvious successor was his grandson, Charles. But by a succession of happy dynastic accidents, Charles had inherited, in addition to the ancestral central European Habsburg lands, the wealthy territories of the Netherlands and the kingdom of Spain. The imperial title would cap unprecedented superpower status, and the pope was not alone in wishing to prevent his getting it. For a time, the seven imperial electors enjoyed immense leverage. One of them was Luther's territorial prince: Elector Frederick 'the Wise' of Saxony. Frederick was thoroughly old-fashioned in religion, but immensely proud of the university he had founded, and of its new superstar professor. He thus protected Martin Luther from his enemies. When Charles (who could pay larger bribes) was duly elected, Luther was summoned under safe conduct to the imperial diet at Worms. In front of the dignitaries Luther refused to recant his errors, proclaiming 'here I stand, I can do no other' – a veritable slogan of individual freedom and modernity. In fact, these words may have been a later gloss on what Luther actually said, a declaration that he would not retract anything, for 'my conscience is captive to the Word of God', a perhaps less appealing motto for moderns. In the aftermath of Worms, Frederick smuggled Luther away to his castle at the Wartburg, where, hidden from the world for nearly a year, he translated the New Testament into powerful and idiomatic German.

In the course of these travails, Luther had become a celebrity, and a German national hero. Humanists (mistakenly) hailed him as one of their own, blowing away the barbarous 'sophistries' of academic theology. Town burghers and rural peasants alike saw in him an icon of resistance to judicial and economic oppression by agents of the Church. He also became in the early 1520s a runaway best-selling author, the J. K. Rowling (or perhaps the Richard Dawkins) of his day. Unlike the writings of Wyclif or Hus, Luther's books and pamphlets were printed. The co-incidence of Luther's protest and the new technology of the printing press seemed to later 16th-century Protestants a veritable providence of God. In fact, printing was not so new. Gutenberg had printed his Latin bible in Mainz almost thirty years before Luther was born, and a well-established printing industry existed in many European cities, with Catholic devotional works the largest category of imprint. Yet Luther's explosion into print marked a momentous turning point in the history of the press, the employment of the printed book for the transmission of opinions, rather than merely knowledge or edification. Here again, the fragmented nature of German society helped. Elsewhere, printing tended to be concentrated in a few towns and cities (in England, nearly all books were produced in London). But in Germany, presses were widely scattered across the empire's many urban centres, making them more difficult for central authority to control.

Zwingli and the beginnings of radicalism

The protest against Rome was not just Luther's affair. He was the prophet, rather than in any concrete sense the leader of the movement, and the Reformation involved discrete reformations from its earliest stages. Events in the Swiss city of Zürich bear this out. The moving figure here was the resident preacher at the principal town church, Huldrych Zwingli (1484–1531), who by his own account 'began to preach the Gospel of Christ in 1516 long before anyone in our region had ever heard of Luther'. Zwingli differed from Luther in having a stronger background in humanism, and a deep acquaintance with the works of Europe's leading Christian humanist, and scourge of obscurantism in the Church, Desiderius Erasmus. This was to be significant for the different directions taken by Luther's and Zwingli's theologies. On the question of authority, Zwingli developed a similar position to Luther's: scripture was the sole basis of truth, and the power of popes and councils was illusory. Zwingli's 'Ninety-Five Theses' moment came in Lent 1522, when he presided over a meal of sausages that ostentatiously breached the rules for abstaining from meat in the run-up to Easter. Christian 'liberty' in such matters was a central plank of Zwingli's, as of Luther's, teaching, and no doubt an important element in its popular appeal. In the aftermath of the sausage incident, Zürich's town council backed Zwingli against the local bishop, and gave him the opportunity to defend his views in a (rigged) public disputation. In 1524, religious images were removed from the city churches, and fasting and clerical celibacy were abolished. In 1525, the Latin mass was replaced with a vernacular communion service. This was a pattern of 'urban reformation' replicated across much of Germany and Switzerland in the 1520s, as mini-Luthers and mini-Zwinglis sprang up to demand reform from the pulpit, and town magistrates, sensing the popular mood, decided to recognize their demands. In Switzerland, however, the pace of change tended to be quicker – the important German cities of Augsburg and Nuremberg, for example, did not unequivocally opt for Lutheranism until the early 1530s.

Change was swift in Zürich, but not quick enough for some. A group around the humanist Konrad Grebel felt that Zwingli was acting too slowly in getting rid of statues of the saints, and broke decisively with him in 1523. Their slogan of 'not waiting for the magistrate' put them at odds with all who wanted the implementation of Reformation to be an orderly and official business. One result of the assault on tradition, and the exaltation of the status of scripture, was to encourage people to read the bible themselves, yet the lessons they drew from it were not always those approved by the leading preachers. Noticing that the practice of baptizing infants was nowhere described in scripture, Grebel began rebaptizing adult members of his group. Zwingli's successor in Zürich, Heinrich Bullinger, would later coin the term 'anabaptists' (rebaptizers) to describe them, a label freely applied by both Catholics and Protestants to all on the radical end of the Reformation spectrum. Luther, meanwhile, was having his own problems with the people he was soon to start calling *schwärmer* – enthusiasts or fanatics. During Luther's enforced absence in the Wartburg over 1521–2, his collaborator Andreas von Karlstadt decided to force the pace of change in Wittenberg, removing images from the churches and celebrating mass in German. Luther approved the ends, but not the way of proceeding, and on his return reversed the changes. Karlstadt became one of Luther's bitterest critics, comparing the gradualist approach to allowing a small child to carry on playing with a sharp knife. Luther accused Karlstadt of having swallowed the Holy Spirit 'feathers and all'. The potability of the Holy Spirit was further signified by the arrival in Wittenberg of the 'Zwickau Prophets', three artisan visionaries ejected from a Saxon cloth town, claiming direct inspiration from God and the imminent end of the world. They had been influenced by the former preacher there, Thomas Müntzer, another militant who decided early on that Luther was a busted flush, and that the 'inner word' of private revelation trumped the 'dead letter' of written scripture.

Popular reformation and the Peasants' War

Luther had sown the wind; now he would reap the whirlwind. So at least his Catholic enemies claimed, arguing that departure from the time-honoured teachings and traditions of the Universal Church would lead inevitably to anarchy and rebellion. Events in the mid-1520s suggested they had a point. Luther was no social revolutionary. His 'liberty' was freedom of the Christian conscience from the spiritually burdensome rules and rituals of late medieval Catholicism, not a renegotiation of the political and economic bonds structuring society. But what is preached and what is heard are not necessarily the same. Perhaps it is not so much that Luther was misunderstood, as that various groups in German society selected from his teachings whatever made sense to them, and applied it to their existing grievances and ambitions. In some places, like Lübeck, Lutheranism became the ideology for a municipal *coup d'état*, adopted by middle-ranking guildsmen previously excluded from town government by rich patricians. Studies of popular printed propaganda for the Reformation – broadsheets and woodcut prints – suggest that serious attempts to get across Luther's more complex theological ideas were usually sacrificed in favour of broad satirical attacks on the Catholic clergy and hierarchy, with monks and friars depicted as ravening wolves, the pope as a ferocious dragon.

For all that the early Reformation is sometimes described as an 'urban event', it was in the countryside and among the peasants (the overwhelming majority of the population) that the teachings of the reformers were most obviously domesticated to an agenda of social and economic aspiration. The peasantry had longstanding grievances against their landlords, both lay nobles and wealthy monasteries, who for decades had been appropriating common land and seeking to intensify the burdens of serfdom. There had been isolated revolts in the later 15th and early 16th centuries, but in 1524–5 the scale and coordination of rebellion was completely unprecedented, constituting what has been described as a 'revolution of the common man'. Beginning in the Black Forest area of southwestern Germany, the revolt spread to the north and east, with further large outbreaks in Switzerland and Austria. The rebels pulled down nobles' castles and sacked monasteries, doing so in the name of 'the Gospel', and demanding the abolition of serfdom, since, according to the Twelve Articles adopted by a combined rebel army, 'Christ has delivered and redeemed us all ... by the shedding of His precious blood'. The relationship between the Peasants' War and the Reformation has been much debated. It was clearest in Thuringia, where the radical preacher Thomas Müntzer himself led a peasant band, believing he was inaugurating the Apocalypse and Second Coming of Christ. Marxist historians – before reunification the revolt was a specialism of East German scholarship – have seen it as a fundamentally secular episode, the peasants expressing economic aspirations in religious terms since they had no other legitimating language available. The sight of his theology transformed into revolutionary ideology horrified Luther, who brought no credit on himself by publishing in May 1525 a pamphlet urging princes to slaughter without compunction the 'robbing and murdering hordes of peasants'. They needed little encouragement: the revolt was crushed with great brutality; Müntzer was tortured and beheaded.

German politics and princely reformation

The Peasants' War was a turning point for reform, and for Germany. Before 1525, the Reformation was a gloriously disorderly popular movement, with aspirations to restructure Christian society. A staple of early pamphlets was the figure of Karsthans, the cocky Lutheran peasant, who out-argues the priests and university dons. After 1525, the Reformation was 'tamed', reform became respectable, and Karsthans disappeared. The dissociation of Lutheranism from social radicalism opened the door for princes to adopt what its adherents now called the 'evangelical' faith. First to do so was Albrecht of Hohenzollern, clerical Grand Master of the Teutonic Knights, a crusading order set up in the 13th century to campaign against the pagan peoples of the Baltic region. By 1525, Albrecht had secularized the order's lands, determined to marry, and reinvented himself as Duke of Prussia. At around the same time Philip of Hesse adopted the cause, as did Frederick the Wise's successor as Elector of Saxony, John 'the Constant'. Princely conversions remained a trickle in the 1520s, but accelerated in the following decade when the greater part of north Germany became officially Lutheran. The powerful Elector of Brandenburg signed up in 1539, and the Elector of the Palatinate in 1546.

In the meantime, official reformations were starting to take place outside of Germany and Switzerland, notably in the Scandinavian kingdoms. After victory in a Danish civil war, Christian III established a Lutheran state in 1536. The following year he imposed Lutheranism on Denmark's vassal kingdom of Norway, though it took a generation and more for the change to be accepted by the Norwegian people. The king of Sweden, Gustav Vasa, was quick off the mark in declaring the Swedish Church independent from Rome in 1527. Yet he never showed much personal enthusiasm for Luther's new theology, and reforms were introduced into Sweden at a snail's place, with no final and emphatic national declaration for the Lutheran faith before 1593. Events in another peripheral European kingdom, England, were in some ways similar. Henry VIII had no time for Martin Luther and the feeling was mutual. For all his deference to properly constituted authority, Luther was spectacularly rude about Henry, calling him a 'damnable and rotten worm' in response to a pro-papal book the king wrote in 1521. Luther's view did not change much, even after Henry had seen his own version of the light: 'Squire Harry means to be God, and do as he pleases', Luther sighed, as Henry married for the sixth time. Wedlock was the touch-paper of Henry's English Reformation. The pope's refusal to allow an annulment of his barren marriage to Katherine of Aragon eventually drove Henry into rebellion, declaring himself 'Supreme Head' of the Church of England in 1534. Henry himself was no evangelical (though some important advisors, like Archbishop Thomas Cranmer, certainly were) but he cheerfully employed 'Word of God' rhetoric to justify radical steps like dissolving the monasteries. Kings, as well as peasants, could select what they fancied from the menu of Reformation ideas.

Within Germany, there was a substantial political obstacle to further expansion of Reformation: the Holy Roman Emperor, Charles V. Charles looked upon himself as the chief defender of Catholic Christendom against its foes. The trouble was, those foes were coming from all directions. North African piracy haunted the western Mediterranean, and in the east, the forces of the Turkish Ottoman Empire seemed in relentless advance, under the brilliant and charismatic sultan Suleyman 'the Magnificent'. In the face of expansionist Islam, compromise at home looked sensible, a view shared by Catholic German princes who considered stable government by heretics preferable to the anarchy unleashed by the Peasants' War. In 1526, the imperial diet at Speyer issued a directive that – until a general council of the Church could convene to settle matters – princely territories and self-governing cities should be free to regulate religious matters as they pleased. The Edict of Worms, condemning Luther, his writings, and all who supported him, was in effect suspended. But intense mistrust remained on all sides, and in 1529 a second Diet of Speyer reinstated the Edict of Worms. Six of the princes present, along with the delegates from fourteen towns, signed a 'protestation' against the diet's decision. Their action created a new proper noun – 'Protestant' – and a new political identity.

Protestants banded together against the fear the empire was about to strike back. Under the leadership of Philip of Hesse and John of Saxony, a defensive alliance was concluded in the Thuringian town of Schmalkalden in 1531. This was a political complement to the Augsburg Confession of the previous year, an agreed statement of core Lutheran doctrine, drawn up by Luther's younger collaborator, Philip Melanchthon. 'Protestants' now shared a name, but they did not all share a platform. Zwingli and the Swiss cities did not adopt the Augsburg Confession, having significant theological reservations, especially over interpretation of the communion service. Several South German towns signed up to a separate 'Confession' of the Strassburg reformer Martin Bucer, though most southern towns trickled into the Lutheran orbit during the 1530s. In the following decade, German Lutheranism nearly met a premature end. In 1546, the year of the death of its founding father, Martin Luther, war broke out between Charles V and the Schmalkaldic League. Charles's brilliant victory at Mühlberg in the spring of 1547 allowed him to dictate terms. The Augsburg Interim of the following year made a handful of concessions to Protestant sensibilities – clerical marriage was allowed, and communion for the laity with both bread and wine. But otherwise it insisted on traditional doctrine and discipline in formerly Lutheran states and 'Reformed' towns. There was an exodus of principled refugees, particularly from the German South, the first of many waves of religious immigration in the Reformation. Some exiles, like Bucer, finished up in England, where Henry VIII's successor, the child-king Edward VI, was the figure-head of a strongly Protestant regime, which, like Churchill's government in 1940, saw itself as standing alone against a European tyranny.

Pride comes before a fall. The magnitude of Charles's victory alarmed the German Catholic princes, who, fearing for their autonomy, backed away from their military alliance. Several Protestant states resumed the offensive in 1552, supported by the French Catholic king, Henry II, who saw an opportunity to make mischief. Charles was driven back to the negotiating table, though disillusioned with life, he left the negotiating to his brother Ferdinand, and shortly afterwards retired to a monastery in Spain. The mandates of the 1555 Peace of Augsburg are usually summed up in the Latin tag, *cuius regio, eius religio* ('whoever your ruler is, that's your religion'). Princes within the empire were free either to retain Catholicism or adopt the Augsburg Confession. Cities could profess Lutheranism on condition of allowing Catholic worship as well. Religious divisions were thus recognized and institutionalized, and the Reformation was saved in Germany. But Lutheranism's hour of crisis had produced deep internal wounds. Melanchthon's willingness to submit to the Augsburg Interim, as well as his apparent sympathy for some aspects of 'Reformed'

Protestantism, antagonized self-appointed guardians of Luther's legacy. Quarrels between 'Philipists' and 'Gnesio-' (or orthodox) Lutherans were finally resolved by the 1577 Formula of Concord, but by now Martin Luther's urgent reformism was ossifying into a rigid doctrinal system, obsessed with theological correctness. Lutheranism was no longer the beating heart of religious reform, and, while the Lutherans were squabbling, the Reformation had undergone a second birth.

Calvin, Geneva, and the Second Reformation

The site of that nativity was an unlikely one: the unprepossessing town of Geneva (population about 10,000), on the western fringe of the Swiss Confederation. Like numerous other small city states, Geneva had opted for the Reformation in the early 1530s, ousting its Catholic bishop with the help of its larger Protestant neighbour, Bern, and an exiled French preacher, Guillaume Farel. In 1536, Farel begged for the assistance of another French religious exile, Jean Calvin, who happened to be passing through Geneva on his way to Basel. Calvin was a lawyer by training, who had followed a conventional academic career (no dramatic thunderstorm episode!) before fleeing France in the wake of a crackdown on Protestant sympathizers in 1534. Unlike Luther, who wrote copious if disorderly autobiography, we know little about Calvin's early life, or his private character and habits. But we know plenty about the contents of his mind. Where Luther was boisterous and inconsistent, Calvin was logical and methodical. Luther's theology was a scatter-gun; Calvin's a sniper's rifle.

Today, only specialists remember the titles of Luther's countless short works, but the essential features of Calvin's thought were all contained in a single volume, *The Institutes of the Christian Religion*, which expanded in various French and Latin versions from an original edition of 1536. The book's full title advertised to readers that it contained 'almost the whole sum of piety and

PROMPTE   ET SINCERE

IOHANNES · CALVINVS ·
ANNO · ÆTATIS · 53 ·
· B ·

2. This 1562 portrait of Calvin at the age of 53 gives few clues about his character or personality

whatever it is necessary to know in the doctrine of salvation'. It was a formidable attempt – using logic, grammar, and rhetoric – to schematize everything that was knowable about an ultimately mysterious and transcendent God.

Calvin's campaign to reform Geneva (Farel soon moved on elsewhere) got off to a rocky start. The city council wanted a Zürich- or Bernese-style reformation, where the magistrates retained complete control over the Church. Calvin favoured cooperation, but insisted on freedom of action, particularly over the issue of excommunicating unrepentant sinners, a task which devolved to the Consistory, a body comprising ministers, magistrates, and lay 'elders', with responsibility for discipline and moral regulation. The campaign against 'sin' involved Calvin in long-running battles with sections of the Genevan social elite, who disliked being told not to dance at society weddings, or give traditional family names (and therefore those of Catholic saints) to their children at baptism. In fact, it took almost two decades for Calvin (who held no official post beyond that of preacher) to stamp his authority on the town. His eventual success owed much to the support of large numbers of refugees who made Geneva their home in the middle decades of the century, more than doubling the population. The great majority, like Calvin himself, were from France. But modern Geneva's reputation as international centre par excellence was anticipated in these years. In the mid-1550s, it gave a home to escapees from the (temporary) Catholic restoration of Henry VIII's pious daughter Mary I. One of these, the Scot John Knox, liked what he saw, considering Geneva 'the most perfect school of Christ that ever was in this earth since the days of the Apostles'. There were other places where Christ was truly preached, but none for 'manners and religion to be so sincerely reformed'. Posterity has been less effusive, inclined to regard Calvinist Geneva as dour and repressive, a theocratic police state. Modern scholarship has tried to redress the balance, emphasizing the Consistory's role in social welfare and even marriage counselling. Nonetheless, 16th-century Geneva was not the European capital of fun.

It was, however, the epicentre of a political and doctrinal earthquake, sending the seismic waves of a 'Second Reformation' right across the European continent. Only to a limited extent did Calvin plan and direct this movement, but he was its patron and godfather. Calvin's most direct influence was on Geneva's huge neighbour to the west, and in the organization and attitudes of the French Protestants who became known, for reasons no one has been able to explain satisfactorily, as Huguenots. French émigré pastors were trained in Geneva and sent back into their homeland; the Genevan presses churned out Protestant books for the French market. Calvin wrote letters of advice on the establishment of consistories, and stern warnings about avoiding contamination from Catholic worship. Huguenot numbers grew rapidly in the middle of the 16th century, especially in the towns, with a concentration of numbers in the south and west; they peaked at somewhere between 10% and 20% of the French population. A minority group, blatantly defying the wishes of the French crown, required a militant and self-righteous ideology, and a tight organizing structure: Calvinism supplied both. Local congregations sent representatives to provincial synods, and a 'national synod' convened in Paris in 1559. But what really gave French Protestantism the potential to destabilize the nation was committed aristocratic support, with all that implied for political leadership and military muscle. Backed by the noble houses of Bourbon, Condé, and Coligny, French Protestants ambitiously imagined they could convert a kingdom. Political instability was compounded by the premature death of Henry II, and attempts by the fervently Catholic Guise family to dominate the regency of Francis II. The result was civil war, or rather, a generation's worth of civil wars which ran in fits and starts from 1562 to almost the end of the century. Earlier scholarship emphasized politics in all of this, but recent studies tend to think the 'French Wars of Religion' were aptly named. They became particularly intense when, due to the failure of all Henry II's sons to reproduce, the Protestant Henry of Bourbon became first heir (1584) and then inheritor (1589) of the kingdom as Henry IV. But France, eldest daughter of the Church, was not ready for a Protestant king. We can add 'Paris is worth a mass' to the list of things famous people are supposed to have said, but didn't. Nonetheless, Henry realized his conversion was the price of political stability. France was the greatest 'might-have-been' of the Reformation era, but after Henry's reconciliation with Rome in 1593, French Protestantism began a slow decline. It was too significant a movement to repress outright, however, and Henry's 1598 Edict of Nantes granted limited rights of worship to Huguenots, institutionalizing the religious divide.

Calvinism played its part in another armed struggle of the later 16th century: that of the Low Countries against Spanish overlordship. The earliest religious dissent in the Netherlands was Lutheran, and ruthlessly suppressed by the government of Charles V. Luther's own opposition to illegal underground congregations, or conventicles, probably didn't help, and over time Calvinist influence increased. The constitutional conflict was not at first obviously religious in complexion. When Charles V abdicated, he divided his dominions: the ancestral lands went (with the imperial title) to his brother, Ferdinand; Spain and the Netherlands to his son, Philip. Whereas Charles (a native of Ghent) understood the Netherlands, with their complex jigsaw of jurisdictions and traditions of local autonomy, the Spanish Philip did not, and began a policy of centralization. The result was open revolt (1566), and an almost universal revulsion, on the part of Catholics as well as Protestants, against the brutal methods of the Duke of Alva's Spanish army sent to repress it. Increasingly, however, Calvinism could paint itself as the creed of patriotic resistance, particularly after it was adopted by the military and political leader of the revolt, William of Orange. Eventually, the Netherlands divided along a religious fault-line. The north espoused Protestantism; the southern 'Spanish Netherlands' became a bastion of Catholicism, later acquiring the name 'Belgium'. There was a curious development in the independent Dutch Republic, however. Calvinism was recognized as the 'public' religion, but never fully became a state church. Ministers had grown used to controlling members of voluntary congregations through the institution of the consistory, and were unwilling to give this up. The result was that while anyone might attend church and hear sermons, actual members of the Calvinist Church, receiving communion, and placing themselves under the authority of the consistory, remained a minority – only about 10% of the population of Holland as late as the end of the 16th century.

Calvinism was a protean beast. It shaped the Reformation in all parts of the British Isles, but produced different shapes in each of them. John Knox returned to Scotland from his Genevan idyll in 1559, and launched a revolution against the pro-French Catholic queen, Mary Stewart, who eventually (1568) fled south to England, leaving her son James to be brought up a godly Calvinist prince. The Scottish Kirk wore its Calvinist heart on its sleeve, setting up a full 'presbyterian' system with consistories (called here kirk sessions), synods, and a General Assembly. In England, by contrast, the later 16th-century Church was a theological hybrid. Its doctrine was more or less solidly Calvinist, but its governing structures were hand-me-downs from the medieval Catholic Church, involving bishops, cathedrals, and diocesan church courts. This had much to do with a historical and doctrinal oddity of the English scene, the 'royal supremacy' established by Henry VIII. Governing the Church though a score of bishops was much easier for the crown than dealing with gaggles of independent-minded ministers in an assembly. The ossification of English Church structures also owed a lot to the conservative outlook of Elizabeth I, who succeeded her Catholic half-sister Mary in 1558. Having restored Protestant worship, ditched the pope, and re-dissolved the monasteries, Elizabeth determined that nothing else should really change over the course of her 45-year reign, despite the urgings of 'Puritans' who wanted the Church of England more closely to resemble the 'best reformed' European churches (i.e. Zürich and Geneva). In Ireland, Protestant Reformation went hand-in-hand with English colonialism, and foundered largely for that reason. In the Tudor period, Irish Protestantism was largely confined to 'New English' settlers, as opposed to the 'Old English', descendants of the 12th-century Anglo-Norman invaders, who, like the Gaelic population, remained stubbornly impervious to the blandishments of the Protestant Gospel. Irish Protestantism developed a strongly Calvinist tinge, suited to the mindset of a group which remained a beleaguered minority even after reinforcement by the 'plantation' of Scots Presbyterians into Ulster in the early years of the 17th century.

The religious and ethnic complexity of Ireland was mirrored on the other side of the continent. Eastern Europe was a patchwork of peoples, in which Calvinists jostled with Catholics, Lutherans, Jews, Orthodox Christians, and (in Ottoman-controlled areas of the southeast) Muslims. Calvinism made some progress among the nobility of Bohemia, though here it had to reach accommodations with the still-powerful native reformism of the Hussites. The Reformation also put down multiple roots in the huge multi-ethnic state created in 1569 by union of the kingdom of Poland with the Grand Duchy of Lithuania. This was the opposite of a strongly centralized state, with an elective monarchy and a powerful noble-dominated parliament, the *Sejm*. In 1562, King Sigismund II exempted landowners from the verdicts of the church courts, effectively allowing them to patronize whatever form of religion they chose. This benefited not only Calvinists, but radical 'Unitarians' who denied the doctrine of the Trinity, and for whom Poland now became a haven. It was, however, in the 'three Hungaries' that Calvinism fared best. The nation was divided by 1541 into a northwestern Habsburg kingdom, a Christian principality of Transylvania (a tributary state of the Ottoman Sultan), and a southern region ruled directly by the Turks. The Ottoman advance greatly assisted Protestantism by destroying the control structures of the Catholic Church: half of Hungary's bishops were slain at the disastrous battle of Mohács in 1526. Uniquely, Transylvania recognized four accepted state religions: Catholic, Reformed, Lutheran, and Unitarian. A pattern throughout the East, however, was that Lutheranism tended to appeal only in pockets of German-speaking communities, while Calvinism had greater saleability among the Poles and Hungarians for whom Germans were historic oppressors.

Calvinism made significant inroads into Lutheran Germany itself, where the Peace of Augsburg had recognized only one alternative to Catholicism. This was a genuine 'Second Reformation', getting underway in 1563 when Elector Frederick III of the Palatinate announced a switch of allegiance for his Lutheran state. Frederick's capital, Heidelberg, site of an important university, became the leading centre of German Calvinism, and the Heidelberg Catechism drafted by two of its professors was used widely throughout the Calvinist world. A number of other petty princes followed suit over the following half century, not always carrying their subjects with them. As elsewhere in Europe, a selling point of the Calvinist system was its malleability. German princely Calvinism had a politically authoritarian style – no synods or general assemblies here. Relations in Germany between Lutherans and Calvinists remained tense at best. But it was Calvinism that stood to the fore in the era's greatest ideological conflict, confrontation with the forces of resurgent Catholicism.

Catholic responses

The revival of the Catholic Church's fortunes is a remarkable, even a surprising story. In around 1560 it seemed the Protestant juggernaut was virtually unstoppable. A northern arc of kingdoms – Sweden, Denmark, Scotland, England – were all lost, and heresy was spreading like wildfire in the previously pious Catholic towns of France and the Netherlands. Across swathes of Eastern Europe, Catholicism was becoming a minority religion, and the Habsburg monarchy appeared unable to preserve the faith in its own backyard: most of the Austrian nobility became Protestant in the third quarter of the century. Germany was a disaster zone, its population perhaps 80% Protestant; the sole remaining Catholic state of any importance was the Duchy of Bavaria. Only in Catholicism's Mediterranean heartlands – Portugal, Spain, and Italy – had the authorities managed to snuff out the flame of Protestantism almost before it had caught light.

If we fast-forward 60 years, the picture looks very different. The Huguenots were defeated and diminishing in France; the southern Netherlands were recovered and re-Catholicized; most of south Germany was back in Catholic hands; and a vibrant Catholic revival was sweeping through Austria, Poland, and Hungary. Protestantism had its back to the wall, and knew it. How had this come about? A cynical answer has something to commend it: military force. In the late 16th and early 17th centuries, the pope really did have a lot of divisions. Ultimately, the Huguenots were the losing side in a civil war, and the recovery of the southern Netherlands was due principally to the brilliant victories in the 1590s of the Spanish general, the duke of Parma. The Habsburgs too began to apply military logic to the religious problems of their territories, after the reigns of some pretty diffident emperors in the second half of the 16th century. But force is by no means the whole story. Catholicism remade itself in the course of its own reformation, drawing on its historic strengths but also exposing itself to the shock of the new. The process began in earnest at the Council of Trent (1545–63).

To reformers of all stripes, a general council had long seemed the solution to the Church's ills. But powerful vested interests had kicked it into the long grass. The French king, Francis I, was obstructionist, aware that his rival Charles V would benefit if a council healed the schism in Germany. The popes themselves feared a revival of the conciliar movement, and a draining away of their authority. The result was that by the time a council actually convened, in the northern Italian town of Trent, religious divisions

3. A 16th-century engraving of the Council of Trent in session: its decisions would set the tone for Catholicism for centuries to come

had run too deep, and the reconciliation with the Lutherans that Charles V hoped for was never really on the agenda. In fact, the Council's early sessions (1545–7) were largely concerned with formulating definitions of Catholic doctrine (for example, on the complementary status of scripture and tradition) in a way that clearly distinguished them from Protestant views. The later sessions (1551–2, 1562–3) tackled institutional reform, ordering bishops to reside in their dioceses as pastors to their flocks, rather than swan around as leisured aristocrats or government officials. Perhaps the most crucial reform was the order for all dioceses to set up seminaries for the training of clergy, a distinctly haphazard process in the Middle Ages. The aspiration for a disciplined and educated priesthood was a cornerstone of Catholic reform.

Trent inaugurated a new way of being Catholic, expressed in the Latinized adjective 'Tridentine'. When the Council wrapped up, the process of Catholic reform still had a long way to go, but the achievements were undeniable. The clarification of Catholic doctrine on virtually all contested issues created a unified template of belief for a single *Roman* Catholic Church, superseding the woollier 'Catholicisms' which had co-existed in pre-Reformation Europe. Trent authorized a standardized catechism (religious instruction book) for the laity, and imposed a uniform order on the celebration of the mass – the Tridentine rite still beloved of Catholic traditionalists. In seeking to eliminate 'abuses', the Council directed the energies of priests and bishops firmly towards the pastoral mission of the Church. Trent also had the opposite result from 15th-century councils, serving to augment rather than diminish the authority of the papacy. Successive popes closely monitored the proceedings, and when Pius IV (1559–65) confirmed the decrees, he reserved to himself their interpretation. Papal authority was enhanced morally as well as institutionally in the aftermath of Trent. There was no going back to the louche atmosphere of Renaissance Rome, exemplified by the disgraceful Borgia pope, Alexander VI. Late 16th-century successors like Pius V (1566–72), Gregory XIII (1572–85), and Sixtus V (1585–90) did much to restore the honour of the papacy through high standards of personal austerity.

In parallel with the Council's deliberations, popes overhauled the central management of the Church. The Congregation of the Holy Office (a papally controlled inquisition) was established in 1542, and a papal 'Index' of forbidden books in 1559, with a Congregation of the Index in 1587 – these are the most notorious examples of 'Counter-Reformation'. 'Congregations' in this sense were committees of cardinals tasked with specified administrative duties. The papacy remained Europe's pre-eminent example of an elective monarchy, but the cardinal-electors (whose number was fixed at 70 by Sixtus V) were taking on the character of an official bureaucracy reporting to the pope, and began less to resemble a class of feuding aristocrats.

One of the Tridentine congregations (established 1622) was that for the propagation of the faith, *Propaganda fide*. The fact that it has given its name to a modern term for political deceit and manipulation is an indication of the cultural prejudices sometimes embedded in etymology. *Propaganda* was a belated official recognition that the Roman Church was no longer a purely European Church. In the wake of Portuguese traders and Spanish conquerors (and frequently in advance of them) Catholicism had become a world religion, the first truly global faith, with adherents in every continent bar Antarctica and the still undiscovered Australia. The evangelization of the wider world was not a direct riposte to the Protestant Reformation. The first missionaries in Mexico were humanist-leaning Franciscan friars who knew little or nothing of Martin Luther. But it soon seemed evident that the harvest of souls in new worlds compensated for their loss in the old. One missionary priest wrote excitedly about Japan in the later 16th century that God 'in the place of so many thousand souls in Upper and Lower Germany who were tempted by the Evil Enemy [the devil] ... has elected another holy people from the other side of the world, who has hitherto known nothing of the holy faith.' In so far as the missionary endeavour beyond Europe was part of the competition between Protestantism and Tridentine Catholicism to assert the identity of a universal and apostle-like Church, the latter had shot dramatically ahead on points.

At the forefront of the Catholic missions were the religious orders, the Franciscans, Dominicans, and Augustinians who had long been the itinerant face of evangelism in Europe. The spiritual fervour of Catholic reformation spawned numerous new religious orders, but none were as significant, at home or overseas, as the Society of Jesus – the Jesuits – founded by the Basque nobleman Ignatius Loyola (1491–1556) in 1534, and ratified by the pope in 1540. Within little more than half a century, Ignatius's handful of ragged companions had mushroomed into an international organization of some 13,000 members. The Jesuits' success was matched only by the deep distrust they aroused, in Catholic as well as Protestant circles – 'Jesuitical' has its cognates in many European languages. Myths about the Jesuits abound: they were not founded to serve as anti-Protestant shock-troops, and they did not take a special vow of 'loyalty' to the pope (rather, a pledge to go on mission anywhere in the world at the pope's command). Their original vocation, and for long their forte, was education. Jesuit schools offered a free education to the poor, and places were also much in demand from social elites (including some Protestants). But the Jesuits were soon drawn into the vanguard of the campaign to recover space and souls from the Reformation – they were active as preachers and confessors across Germany and Poland, and as missionaries (occasionally plotters) in Sweden and the British Isles. The unique Jesuit 'ethos' came from a marriage between traditional monastic structures and flexible activism (members were not bound to recite the 'hours' together in common). It also reflected the influence of a remarkable book, Ignatius's *Spiritual Exercises* – a 'how-to' manual of interiorized and imaginative prayer, which created the modern concept of the 'retreat'. The Jesuits' instinct was to reform society from the top down, and they were drawn to the orbit of social elites. The devout Habsburg emperor Ferdinand II (r. 1619–37) had a Jesuit confessor, Guillaume Lamormaini, who stiffened Ferdinand's mood of increasing militancy towards his Protestant subjects.

The Thirty Years War and after

The numerous regional confrontations between Reformation and Counter-Reformation were after 1618 subsumed into a general and bloody conflagration, pitting the Spanish and Austrian Habsburgs, and a Catholic League headed by Duke Maximilian of Bavaria, against the Protestant states of Germany, the Netherlands, and Scandinavia (James I's England, to the dismay of Puritans, held aloof). The Thirty Years War began as a war of religion, though it didn't end that way. The initial flash-point was that old cockpit of religious contention, Bohemia, and the attempt of Bohemian rebels to replace the then Archduke Ferdinand as their overlord with the Calvinist Elector Frederick of the Palatinate. Frederick's catastrophic defeat in 1620 at the battle of the White Mountain overturned two centuries of Bohemian religious experiment: the Hussite Church was eliminated, and its pastors, along with newer Protestant associates, were expelled. Shortly afterwards, Catholic League forces sacked Heidelberg. A string of German victories through the 1620s encouraged Ferdinand to impose a radical and arbitrary settlement. His Edict of Restitution (1629) demanded the return of all Church lands and bishoprics secularized in Germany since 1552; it also reasserted an almost complete prohibition on Calvinism in the Empire.

The Edict was a step too far: it alienated moderate allies, pushed Calvinists and Lutherans into cooperating with one another, and provoked an extraordinary military intervention. The king of Sweden, Gustavus Adolphus, invaded Germany wearing the mantle of a Protestant saviour. His stunning victory at Breitenfeld in 1631 reversed the course of the war, and though Gustavus was killed in battle the following year, military equilibrium in Germany was stabilized, and Ferdinand began to explore avenues of compromise. Meanwhile, fearful of Habsburg hegemony in Europe, the wily Cardinal-Minister Richelieu brought Catholic France into the war on the 'Protestant' side. The studied neutrality of the anti-Spanish Pope Urban VIII also made it more difficult to see the war in its last stage as primarily one of religion.

The Reformation in Germany fought itself to a standstill, and a series of agreements known collectively as the Treaty of Westphalia (1648) ended the conflict, though France and Spain would fight each other till 1659. In a triumph of pragmatism over principle, Westphalia stabilized the confessional map by accepting the religious *status quo ante* (1624 was picked as point of reference, to annul the Edict of Restitution). The independence of Protestant Holland was formally recognized, as was the Habsburg *coup de main* in the east. Within the empire, Calvinism was at last given full legal recognition, and, in a striking innovation, Lutheran subjects in Catholic territories, and Catholics in Lutheran lands, were granted the right to worship quietly at home 'without investigation or disturbance'.

While the Thirty Years War was entering its last phases, the British decided to indulge in their own round of private religious warfare. The differences between the state churches of England and Scotland were magnified after Charles I ascended to the throne of both kingdoms, and prescribed a more ceremonialist, 'high' style of Protestant worship for the Church of England. The attempt to extend it to the Scottish Kirk provoked rebellion, and the signing of a National Covenant (1638) to protect the principles of the Reformation. In 1641, Catholic rebels in Ireland turned with marked ferocity on perceived oppressors in their midst, and news of massacres encouraged paranoid fears in England that Charles was being secretly manipulated by a cabal of Catholic advisors. The English Civil War that erupted in 1642 pitted constitutionalism against unfettered monarchical power, but it had a strongly religious flavour. The defeat and subsequent execution of Charles (1649) allowed Puritans to implement their long frustrated plans for full 'godly' reformation, and also unleashed a wave of popular religious creativity in the form of new radical sects – of these, the Baptists and Quakers would survive the longest. The restoration of Charles II in 1660 restored a kind of political stability but it could not recork the shaken bottle of religious unity. 'Non-conformists' were now permanently separated from the Church of England, whose adherents were beginning to describe themselves as 'Anglicans' – a rather different sort of Protestant from established continental varieties.

It is usually asserted that in the second half of the 17th century the role played by faith commitments in international and domestic politics was on the wane, and that the era of religious wars, the era of Reformation itself, was over. This is true up to a point: the political colossus of the age was Louis XIV of France (r. 1656– 1715), and the coalitions ranged against his expansionist ambitions

4. An allegory of the Revocation of the Edict of Nantes: Louis XIV
oversees Truth unmasking Heresy while (in the roundels) Calvinists
abjure their faith and Catholics destroy a Protestant chapel

brought the former standard-bearer of conviction politics – Catholic Austria – into alliance with Protestant states.

But Louis was at the time firmly identified with the Catholic cause, both by the local Catholic minority who welcomed his invasions of the Netherlands, and by the now fervently anti-Catholic English, who in 1688 deposed their own king, James II, for adherence to popery. Three years before that, Louis had given an astonishing demonstration of the convergence of political absolutism and religious triumphalism, revoking the Edict of Nantes which for almost a century had allowed Huguenots the right to worship in France.

The outcome was repression and rebellion, a wave of expulsions and insincere conversions, and a movement of exiles across borders to nurse bitterness and stoke the fears of their hosts. For a century and a half, reformations had been the chief motor of European political and cultural life. They had not quite exhausted that function, as the age of Enlightenment dawned.

Chapter 2
Salvation

On 31 October 1999, anniversary of the nailing of the Ninety-Five Theses to the door of Wittenberg Castle Church, representatives of the Roman Catholic Church and the Lutheran World Federation assembled in the German city of Augsburg signed a joint declaration stating that 'a consensus in basic truths of the doctrine of justification exists between Lutherans and Catholics'. The Reformation, it seemed, was finally over. Luther and Loyola may have been smiling benignly down from heaven; more likely they were turning in their respective graves.

'Justification' is the theologians' description for how sinful men and women become acceptable in the eyes of God and consequently qualify to share eternal life with him in heaven. The Reformation was, first and foremost, a protracted argument about the rules and mechanisms of salvation. The Christian metanarrative hinges on two fixed points of reference. Humanity lost the friendship of God through an act of primordial rebellion: the 'Fall' of Adam and Eve introduced sin into the world, an 'original sin' that marked and stained the natures of their descendants henceforth. But God himself took the initiative in restoring that friendship, assuming a human identity in Christ, who, in an ultimate act of love and sacrifice, suffered death on the cross and 'atoned' for Adam's sin. The door to Salvation, shut in the

Garden of Eden, was potentially open once more. This much was agreed by all mainstream thinkers of the Reformation era. Contention raged over how individual Christians might actually proceed through that door, the role of the Church in preparing them to do so, and whether the door was open for all or just for a few.

Justification and faith

It is a common misconception, among ordinary Catholics as well as Protestants, that the Catholic Church taught or teaches that heaven can be earned by the performance of 'good works'. Salvation, as the great theologian St Augustine (354–430) had insisted, was not a right but a response to an invitation. Medieval Catholic theology held that God freely and on his own initiative offered 'grace' to sinners: grace can be defined as the unmerited favour extended by God to humans, making them capable of enjoying eternal life. People became justified when they accepted the offer of grace, and demonstrated that acceptance by performing the good works God's commandments demanded of them.

The tricky thing was knowing whether one had done enough to count as an unqualified 'yes' to God's invitation. Late medieval academic theology reassured people God would never demand from them more than they were capable of giving. The teaching was summed up in an adage of the German theologian Gabriel Biel (d. 1495): *facere quod in se est* ('do what is in you'). But could people ever feel truly certain that they, like Boy Scouts, had done their best? One theory holds there was a widespread and morbid 'salvation anxiety' in late medieval society, manifested in an intense, hyperactive, performance of piety. Much evidence suggests that lay people gave generously to the building and refurbishing of churches, and were avid in veneration of saints, attendance at masses, going on pilgrimage, and purchasing of indulgences. Perhaps what has been called the 'guiltification' of late medieval

Christians was reaching breaking point. But it is possible to read developments in a more healthy and positive light. Such characteristic features of pre-Reformation piety as the flourishing of local saints' cults, and the formation of religious brotherhoods or confraternities, suggest the laity's desire for more involvement and control over the practice of their faith, as well as a strong recognition of religion's communal significance.

Luther, however, is the definitive case-study in late medieval Catholic 'scrupulosity'. The young monk was tortured by a sense of unworthiness, and of the futility of his monkish efforts to win the favour of God. The crisis was resolved, perhaps in a moment of breakthrough and illumination in a monastic upper room – what Luther later called his 'Tower Experience' – more likely, as a result of gradual conviction between about 1513 and 1518. The catalyst was the biblical writings of St Paul, and in particular his statement (Romans 1:17) that 'the righteous shall live by faith'. Luther liberated himself from a spiral of anxiety and self-loathing when he decided that the righteousness justifying a Christian before God was not achieved, but *imputed* – that is, as a result of Christ's sacrifice on the cross, God chose to accept individuals as righteous, even though they remained entirely sinful. The whole sum of the Old and New Testaments, the Law, and the Gospel, was encapsulated in this insight. The paradoxical point of God's commandments was to be impossible to fulfil, to convince humans of their own worthlessness, so they could receive the 'good news' that God would accept them anyway if they simply trusted, had faith in, his promises. Hence, the Lutheran doctrine of 'Justification by Faith' (and in his bible translation of 1522 Luther did not scruple to add the word 'alone' to St Paul's conclusion that 'a man is justified by faith without the deeds of the law'). Salvation was no longer the end goal of a truly Christian life, but rather its starting point.

Could common folk, without theological training, understand what Luther was proposing? It would be patronizing to insist they could not, and also difficult to account for the enthusiasm with which the message was received, even if, for many, the 'liberation' promised by the gospel was a social and political rather than psychological or spiritual one. We can, however, only fully make sense of this reception if we remember that Luther was a late medieval Catholic, not a 'Protestant', and that the early Reformation was a movement within early 16th-century Catholicism rather than an attack on it from outside. For all the glorious untidiness of relics and saints' cults, the predominant feature of late medieval piety was its intense 'Christocentrism', a devotional concentration on the person and sufferings of Jesus, often depicted in art and text as the 'man of sorrows' sharing the afflictions and miseries of human existence. Revolutionary as it was, Luther's 'theology of the cross' struck a strong cultural chord.

It also raised a fundamental philosophical issue. What role remained for free will in the most crucial question of individual human destiny? Were people free to accept or reject God's offer of salvation? Luther's refusal to entertain the idea, along with his denigration of exalted notions of human dignity more generally, exposed the fragility of the Reformation's alliance with Catholic humanism. Erasmus may well have, in a 16th-century proverbial saying, 'laid the egg which Luther hatched'. But he came to see that a cuckoo had entered his nest. In 1525, Erasmus broke publicly with Luther over the question of the freedom of the will, which, in line with traditional Catholic teaching, he believed to be compatible with God's foreknowledge of future events. Two decades later, Trent solidified the principal doctrinal division of the Reformation when it declared that although justification starts as a completely free gift from God, there is a need for individuals to respond cooperatively, and so a positive role for free will. Whereas Luther's justified sinner remained just that, Trent taught that intrinsic to justification was an individual's actual transformation through grace into a more perfect disciple of Christ. Interestingly, most subsequent Protestant reformers showed considerably more concern than Luther did with the sequel to justification: 'sanctification' of the Christian.

Predestination

Justification by faith was the fault-line between Catholic and Protestant worlds, but a refinement and extension of the doctrine became a lasting marker of difference within the Protestant camp itself. In one sense of the term, 'predestination' was a fairly uncontentious Christian notion, with its roots in the theology of Augustine. God wills, and therefore is cause of, the salvation of those to whom he has made his offer of grace. But what of a less palatable corollary: does God positively will the damnation of the souls who descend to hell? Luther skirted around 'double predestination', but Calvin, logical and comprehensive as ever, did not. Although the idea of predestination came to be indelibly associated with him, Calvin treated it fairly lightly in the first edition of the *Institutes*, lending it increasing prominence only in the face of Catholic and Protestant attacks. It was, in fact, Calvin's successor at Geneva, Theodore Beza (1519–1605), who gave the idea its final and polished form, deciding that God had decreed the eternal destiny of every human soul since before the creation of the world and the fall or 'lapse' of Adam, a doctrine marching under the imposing banner of 'supralapsarian predestinarianism'.

A further logical refinement was that Christ could not have died for all, but for the 'elect' only: a 'Limited Atonement'. Why had God done this, and why, apparently randomly, had he chosen some and rejected others? Because he wanted to: predestination was the ultimate symbol of the utter transcendence, majesty, and freedom from imagined human constraints of the Calvinist God. Catholic critics charged that it made God into a tyrant, and some later 16th-century Lutherans more or less agreed. Backtracking from Luther's own position, they argued that predestination was indeed based on divine foreknowledge of human behaviour. A similar stance was adopted by a Dutch Calvinist 'heretic', Jacobus Arminius (1559–1609), whose views precipitated a schism within the Dutch Reformed Church, and were firmly slapped down by a 1619 Synod at Dordrecht (Dort), attended by international Calvinist representatives. Nonetheless, 'Arminian' doctrine infected the Calvinist Church of England in the early 17th century, and by century's end had become its dominant theology. Even non-conformist Protestant groups – Baptists, and later on Methodists – split into Calvinist and Arminian branches.

Many Christians, then as now, found double predestination an unappetizing doctrine, but for others it was a source of immeasurable comfort. Though it was not possible to know certainly who was saved and who was damned, Calvinist believers were encouraged to seek for signs of 'assurance' in themselves: piety, sobriety, and upright living were likely markers of elect status (God allowing good fruit to be produced by healthy trees), whereas drunkards and fornicators were letting the cat of their eternal destiny out of the bag of their worthless earthly existence. Calvinism thus reinforced social solidarities – it shored up the identity of the 'respectable' against the disreputable (though we should be wary of translating this too narrowly into socio-economic terms: there were poor Calvinists as well as middle-class ones). By dividing both this world and the next into 'them and us' – with the 'them' certainly outnumbering the faithful few – Calvinism stiffened the resolve of rebel minorities in France and the Netherlands, and of exiles and immigrants in many other places. Predestinarian teaching was the rock of the resolute. But for the neurotic or naturally depressive it could be a psychological knife-edge. The early 17th-century London Puritan and diarist Nehemiah Wallington was so haunted by the fear he might be damned that he attempted suicide on no fewer than seventeen occasions.

Predestinarian attitudes were not necessarily Calvinist, or even Protestant. In the 17th century, Catholic Europe, particularly France, housed the phenomenon of Jansenism – a kind of Catholic Puritanism. Its origins lay in an attack by the Dutch theologian

Cornelius Jansen (1585–1638) on the Jesuit Luis de Molina, for teaching that God's foreknowledge of human good works did not take away their free character. Jansenism shared with Calvinism a very negative view of the human capacity for goodness, teaching that grace was completely unmerited. Its most famous exponent was the theologian and mathematician Blaise Pascal (1623–62), scourge of Jesuits, whose *Pensées* present faith, not philosophical reason, as the grounds for knowledge of God. Politically, French Jansenism tended towards 'Gallicanism', the view that the French Church should be independent in practical matters from control by Rome. Not surprisingly, popes condemned the movement, but a streak of Jansenism continued to run through French, and other European, Catholicisms across the 18th century. Too intellectual, and too morally austere, ever to become a significant popular movement, its presence serves as a reminder against viewing Catholicism as a 'monolith', and of the curious directions reformation could take.

The authority of scripture

Heaven can sometimes wait. Intertwined with Reformation debates about the order and causes of salvation were disagreements about where a Christian could find dependable guidance on how to live a life pleasing to God in the meantime. This was, in an authoritarian age, principally an argument about authority. Catholics appealed to the authority of the Church; Protestants to that of the bible. Polemics on the question resembled a theological version of the chicken-and-egg conundrum: which came first, the Church or the bible? Catholics pointed out that Jesus had founded a community, not written a book. Protestants countered that Christ himself was 'The Word', whose presence was experienced through the reading, preaching, and hearing of scripture.

Protestant mythology has the reformers 'discovering' the bible, as if it had lain mouldering and forgotten at the back of a cupboard.

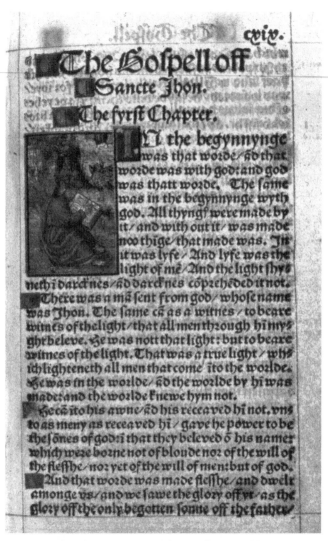

The Gospell off Sancte Jhon.

The fyrst Chapter.

IN the begynnynge was that worde/ & that worde was with god: and god was thatt worde, The same was in the begynnynge wyth god. All thynges were made by it/ and with out it/ was made noo thige/ that made was. Jn it was lyfe/ And lyfe was the light of me/ And the light shyneth i darcknes/ & darcknes coprehedeth it not.

There was a mã sent from god/ whose name was Jhon. The same cã as a witnes/ to beare witnes of the light/ that all men through hi myght beleve. He was nott that light: but to beare witnes of the light. That was a true light/ whych lighteneth all men that come ito the worlde. He was in the worlde/ & the worlde by hi was made: and the worlde knewe hym not.

He cã ito his awne/ & his receaved hi not. vns to as meny as receaved hi/ gave he power to be the sones of god: i that they beleved õ his name: which were borne not of bloude nor of the will of the flesshe/ nor yet of the will of men: but of god.

And that worde was made flesshe/ and dwelt amonge vs/ and we sawe the glory off yt/ as the glory off the only begotten sonne off the father/

5. The opening of St John's Gospel from William Tyndale's printed bible of 1526, offering reassurance to Protestants that 'In the beginning was the Word'

Medieval Christianity was in fact intensely, voraciously biblical, and the scriptures were looked upon by theologians as an encyclopaedia of all useful knowledge. Nor is it true that there were no pre-Reformation vernacular translations for the laity, though England was a significant exception in this respect, the 15th-century Lollards' appeal to their own translations against the traditions of the Church having frightened the bishops into a blanket ban. A further misconception, still regularly wheeled out, is that reformers wanted people to read the bible in order to interpret its meaning for themselves. Reformers believed there was a 'plain truth' of scripture, evident to all right-thinking people, but they took no chances. Luther's German bible, like others of the age, was hedged about with prefaces and marginal glosses to direct the reader. Scripture-reading Christians in the 16th century who made up their own minds about such matters as the Trinity, the divinity of Christ, or infant baptism were condemned by Protestant and Catholic authorities alike. Nonetheless, Protestantism was the religion of the bible, and the bible was the religion of Protestants. Printed in innumerable editions, and in countless languages, the bible became in the 16th and 17th centuries the principal cultural icon of Protestantism, and – in contrast to Catholic societies – was widely found in private homes. Its cultural influence was vast: there are, for example, nearly 70 biblical references in *Henry IV, Part II*, one of Shakespeare's less obviously religious plays.

The Word was to be heard as well as read, so Protestantism was not the sole preserve of the literate. Preaching in the Middle Ages was widespread and popular, but left largely in the hands of the specialists, the friars. By contrast, 'preacher' was almost a synonym for a Protestant minister. Through listening to sermons, the theory went, people would be brought to an awareness of their sins, an acceptance of God's gift of justifying faith, and an assurance of their salvation. Thus, Calvinist preachers, a little incongruously, claimed they were 'saving souls'. The sermon became the focal point of regular Protestant worship, a weekly (in Geneva, a daily) event, and pulpits had pride of place in Protestant churches. In modern secular society, 'sermon' has become a kind of cultural shorthand for tedium. But we should not underestimate the ability of skilled preachers to move and captivate an audience. Those who read from a text were frowned upon: a preacher worth his salt spoke extemporaneously for the full period measured by turning the hour-glass on the pulpit rim. In the battle for souls, the Church of the Catholic Reformation similarly understood the value and importance of preaching: the Jesuits were skilled exponents, and elaborately carved pulpits graced many Baroque churches.

Sacraments

If Catholics did not neglect preaching, neither did Protestants despise sacraments. In the catechism attached to the Anglican Book of Common Prayer, a sacrament was described as 'an outward and visible sign of an inward and spiritual grace'. Catholics might have found definition broadly acceptable, though they would have gibbed at that word 'sign': to them, sacraments were the ordinary and instrumental channels of God's grace to humanity. There was no doubt on any side, however, that sacraments were gifts of the Creator, not man-made rituals. Reformation debates over the sacraments, though they may seem arcane to us, were protracted and bitter because to grasp sacramental theology correctly was to understand God's intentions for mankind. They also reveal the extent to which the Reformation was a 'ritual process', deeply concerned with the symbolic ordering of society for collective as well as individual salvation. And they were bound up, inextricably, with the spiritual authority of the clergy.

Catholic tradition (certified at Trent) fixed the number of sacraments at seven. Five of these were 'life-cycle' rituals, sanctifying the journey from cradle to grave: baptism, confirmation, marriage (and its alternative, ordination to the priesthood), and the anointing of the dying. Two were regular sources of renewable grace: penance (involving confession to, and absolution by, a priest) and the eucharist or holy communion. Penance and the eucharist came as a pair. Medieval Catholics attended mass weekly, but they usually received communion only at Easter, and a prerequisite of reception was confession of sins to a priest. Protestant reformers found themselves unable to accept that all these sacraments had been directly instituted by Christ, and they rationalized the list. In fact, only two survived – baptism and the eucharist, originating in Christ's baptism in the River Jordan and his celebration of the Last Supper on the eve of his crucifixion. Luther initially retained penance as well, then relegated it to the status of a desirable add-on.

As the ceremony of initiation, baptism was foundational to Christian life and to the configuration of church and society. Catholic teaching was that the water of baptism 'washed away' the stain of original sign, making the child a Christian and rendering it eligible for eternal life. A corollary was that infants dying unbaptized were excluded from burial in consecrated ground, and that their souls were denied access to heaven. The eternal damnation of newborns being a step too far for even the severest of theologians, the Church substituted for hell in this case an intermediate 'limbo', where souls suffered no torments. Reformed theology regarded limbo, along with purgatory, as an unscriptural fiction. The idea that baptism was essential for salvation also contradicted and limited God's free choice in predestination. Calvinists valued baptism, but as a confirmation of grace and a token of the faith of the parents and the community. Luther, despite justification by faith, and a conviction that the mark of original sin was indelible, continued to regard baptism as necessary for salvation. Provision for emergency baptism – even, in some circumstances, by midwives – was retained in the Lutheran churches, not least because there was a continued popular demand for it. Lutherans and Calvinists were united, however, in insisting on the practice of *infant* baptism, despite the fact there was no explicit warrant for it in the bible. Their reasoning, which was undoubtedly correct, was that the Church would simply fall apart without it. The more consistently biblical lay theology of the anabaptists, making baptism a voluntary profession of faith by adults, not only diminished the sacral power of the clergy. It deconstructed the Church as a universal social institution, making membership 'opt-in', sectarian, and minoritarian (in the way it has become, ironically enough, for all the mainstream churches in modern Western Europe).

The authority of the clergy was equally at stake in the changes to penitential practice. Hearing confessions provided medieval parish priests with an opportunity for individual regulation and pastoral oversight of parishioners, for testing religious knowledge and dishing out spiritual advice. Reformed Protestantism abandoned the practice, though Calvinist ministers sometimes wistfully felt they had thrown out the baby with the bathwater, and optimistically encouraged lay people to come to them for private 'conferring'. Lutheranism, in this as in other respects more conservative, retained confession, aware of its utility not just for what historians cynically call 'social control', but for peacemaking within the community. The Catholic Reformation meanwhile sought to instil more regular and dutiful observance of a traditional obligation, though there was a noteworthy innovation, the invention in later 16th-century Italy of the closed and screened confessional box. This was promoted by the reforming archbishop of Milan, Carlo Borromeo, and soon diffused throughout the Catholic world. Designed to prevent abuses (such as improper contact between priests and female penitents), the confessional may have helped to foster a more interiorized sense of conscience, guilt, and sin, a Catholic counterpart to the earnest soul-searching of godly Protestants.

No sacrament was the focus of such intense controversy as the eucharist. There was no getting around it: Christ had instructed his disciples (and by extension, his followers throughout time) to 'do this in memory of me', when he had broken and distributed bread at the Last Supper. He had also told them, amazingly, that 'this is my body'. Reformation theologians scrutinized those four words, and argued furiously over the precise meaning of each one of them. Catholic eucharistic understanding remained consistent across the late medieval and Reformation periods. The ceremony of the mass, at which the eucharist was performed, was a sacrifice; in fact, an ongoing re-enactment in time of Christ's sacrifice of himself upon the cross, and thus an immensely powerful 'work' which could be directed towards particular specified ends, such as the relief of souls in purgatory. At the same time, the mass was a source of unparalleled grace for participants. When the priest standing at an altar repeated the 'words of institution' (this is my body), God became literally, physically present, the bread and wine ceasing to be earthly foodstuffs and becoming the body and blood of Christ. By an application of Aristotelian logic which distinguished between the 'accidents', or outward forms of a thing, and its 'substance', or true nature, theologians called the process 'transubstantiation'. But theologians and common folk alike knew that it was an everyday miracle, in which faith was called upon to rise above the evidence of the senses. At the climactic moment, the priest held aloft the consecrated 'host' (from Latin, *ostia*: victim), and the people gazed upon it and adored.

The most sacred of all rituals for Catholics was the most offensive to Protestants. Christ's sacrifice was a once-for-all event, and the idea that it could be replayed through the agency of a priest was the blackest blasphemy. Transubstantiation, with its liftings from pagan philosophy, was a scholastic nonsense, but hardly a harmless one, since it seduced people into worshipping a piece of bread – idolatry. Among early reformers, Zwingli offered the most radical critique and restructuring of the eucharist. Drawing on a humanist tradition of textual analysis, Zwingli concluded that Christ's words were to be understood metaphorically, his 'is' meaning 'symbolizes'. The communion was a pledge of fidelity from God, a powerful token like a wedding ring, but not an actual epiphany. It was also a commemorative event, designed to recall

6. Adrien Ysenbrandt's 1532 painting *The Mass of St Gregory* reinforces teaching on transubstantiation in its depiction of a vision of Christ upon the altar experienced by an early medieval pope

that Last Supper in Jerusalem, and so plain bread, rather than special wafers, was distributed to the communicants, along with the wine that – for fear of spilling the sacred species – had been withheld from the medieval laity. But Luther had no more time for humanist evasions than he did for the scholastic subtleties of transubstantiation. Christ had said 'this is my body', and he must have meant it: 'if he were to order us to eat shit I would do it'. Luther's eucharistic teaching is sometimes described as *consubstantiation* – actual bread and wine remains alongside a real presence of Christ, though this is a term he never used. From the outset, an inability to agree about the nature of Christ's presence, or non-presence, in the eucharist was the main stumbling-block to Protestant unity, and the principal stimulus to the formation of separate 'Lutheran' and 'Reformed' traditions in Germany and Switzerland. Philip of Hesse arranged a meeting between Luther and Zwingli at Marburg in 1529 to heal the rift. On arriving, Luther wrote *'Hoc est corpus meum'* (this is my body) in chalk across the negotiating table. Enough said.

Calvinism had a somewhat 'higher' view of the eucharist than Zwingli's commemorative one. Christ was really and truly present at the sacrament, not materially in the bread and wine, but in the souls of the elect when they worthily received the same – the so-called 'receptionist' view. But all Reformed Protestants celebrated 'the Lord's Supper' with reverence and solemnity, usually four times a year (in contrast to the daily medieval mass), and gathered around a wooden table rather than in front of a stone altar.

7. An English woodcut from the 1570s shows Protestant men and women gathered around a simple communion table, and receiving wine as well as (ordinary) bread

Taking communion was a powerful spiritual experience for participants, but it was at the same time, throughout the Protestant and Catholic worlds, a deeply social act. The right to receive was a symbolic assertion of adult membership of the community, and it was dependent upon being 'in charity' with one's neighbours. The order in which people communicated also reflected social precedence within the community: a few post-Reformation English parishes went so far as to use two different grades of communion wine, with cheap stuff for the hoi polloi. All this was no accident; by longstanding convention, the body of Christ was pre-eminent metaphor for Christian society as a whole, bonded together in (differentiated) unity. It is sadly ironic that through the reformations, the eucharist became and remains a key source of Christian *disunity*, attitudes to it serving as markers of 'confessional' identity. A hallmark of Tridentine Catholicism was intensified public devotion to the consecrated host, carried in public procession on its feast day of Corpus Christi, or displayed and adored in churches in the new 'Forty Hours' devotion.

Apocalypse soon

Salvation had a larger dimension than the fate of the individual, or even of the local community. The Christian narrative sketched at the beginning of this chapter has a conclusion: the Second Coming of Christ, the End of the World, and the creation of a New Heaven and New Earth – events prophesied, in spectacularly opaque imagery, in the biblical book of Revelation, or in Greek, Apocalypse. That book also provided a timetable, of sorts. After being bound for a thousand years, a demonic cosmic adversary of Christ – the Antichrist – was to be loosed onto the world, leading to a final battle between the forces of good and evil, Armageddon.

There was also a promise to the faithful of a thousand-year reign with Christ on earth, a millennium, preceding destruction of the world and the resurrection of the bodies of the dead. Millennial

8. Albrecht Dürer's series of woodcuts on the Apocalypse illustrates
the hold the intense imagery of the Book of Revelation had on late
medieval and early modern imaginations. Note the pope (in three-
tiered tiara) at bottom-right

reveries had fuelled the anarchy of the Peasants' War, and the violent preaching of Thomas Müntzer, but an intense interest in the coming end of the world was not, as today (in Europe, at least), a prerogative of cranks on the fringes of conventional religion. Luther himself was convinced he was living 'in the shadow of the chaos of the Last Days'. He was equally convinced about the identity of the shadowy Antichrist whose machinations were starting to reach a crescendo – not a person, but an institution, the papacy of Rome. The identification became a staple of Reformation thinking, still adhered to in some dark corners of the Protestant world, in Ulster and the United States. The history of the world came to be interpreted as an apocalyptic struggle between the forces of light and darkness, Protestantism and Catholicism, into which events like the French Wars of Religion, or the defeat of the Spanish Armada in 1588, were easily slotted. Set-backs in the face of the Counter-Reformation were explicable: Antichrist was allowed his head for a while, but final victory was assured. Protestant apocalyptic fervour reached its peak with the outbreak of the Thirty Years War in 1618. But the compromises and conclusion of that messy conflict ultimately drew much of its sting. Millenarian expectation was not extinct in the later 17th century, but its slow passage out of the religious mainstream can be regarded as another marker of the passing of the Reformation era.

Chapter 3
Politics

When, in 2003, the then British prime minister, Tony Blair, was asked during a magazine interview a question about his religious beliefs, his leading advisor brusquely interrupted proceedings: 'I'm sorry, we don't do God.' Though politicians elsewhere in the democratic world (particularly the United States) are less reticent to talk about faith than they are in the UK, it is widely taken for granted in modern Western society that 'religion' and 'politics' are intrinsically separable spheres. Faith is understood to be private, not public, and represents the cultural property of specific groups and individuals, not the ordering principle of social and political association. Many Westerners find refusal or inability to distinguish between religion and politics (such as in parts of the contemporary Islamic world) both baffling and menacing. The Reformation is central to the story of how politics and religion began to come apart in European society, yet at the same time it witnessed the flowering of more intense and explicit synthesis between them. The political authorities of 16th- and 17th-century Europe most certainly did 'do God'. Kings ruled in his name, and both they and (most of the time) their subjects accepted that the distribution of political power within society was not a matter of mere historical accident or agreed secular convention. Authority and hierarchy were divinely ordained, a dim earthly reflection of a perfect heavenly society, and an insight into the mind of God. Royal coronations were overtly sacral occasions: like priests, sovereigns were 'anointed' with sacred oil. The invoking of divine sanction on political power was a old theme, foundational to medieval European culture. But the Reformation supplied it with a new impetus, and with new, potentially corrosive, challenges. For what was the appropriate response to a state power professing the 'wrong' religion? The emerging and competing identities of the Reformation era were from the outset enmeshed in vital ways with political processes, making relations between states, and between rulers and subjects, more explicitly ideological than they had ever been. The Reformation was, in fact, the first great era of ideological politics, and in the 16th and 17th centuries, ideology meant religion.

Church-making and state-building

We can begin by reminding ourselves of a sobering fact. The single most important determinant of religious allegiance in the Reformation was neither the enticing appeal of the new Gospel, nor the reassuring draw of the sacraments of the Catholic Church. The religious map of divided Western Christendom was fundamentally decided – in a universal extension of the German principle of *cuius regio, eius religio* – by the wishes of the powers-that-be. After initial ferments and enthusiasms, the Protestant Reformation ultimately triumphed where established governments encouraged or permitted it to, and it failed where they did not. There were, admittedly, important exceptions to this rule. In the Netherlands, an independent Protestant state was forged in the course of a national resistance struggle against the legitimate dynastic ruler, Philip II of Spain. In Scotland, a Calvinist Kirk achieved dominance in spite of the wishes of a Catholic queen, Mary Stewart. Conversely, in Ireland, the attempts of successive Tudor and Stuart governments to impose Protestantism on the nation foundered in the face of popular apathy and sporadic bouts of resistance. Nonetheless, elsewhere the pattern largely holds good. The religious 'frontier' eventually stabilized along a roughly geographic line, but it is important to abandon the inherited notion that Northern Europe was somehow destined to be Protestant; the South condemned to remain Catholic. Scholars used to think, in an unconscious objectification of their own cultural prejudices, that the triumph of the Reformation in England was simply inevitable, and that Mary Tudor's attempts to reverse it in the 1550s were a doomed attempt to swim against the tide of history. Yet it is now widely recognized that foundations for long-term Catholic revival were laid during Mary's reign, and that it was the queen's premature death, not the religious DNA of the English people, that ensured the country's future would be a Protestant one. It would be equally fallacious to attribute the failure of the Reformation in Spain to any national genetic predisposition for fiestas, Holy Week processions, and the cult of the Virgin Mary. Here, the first stirrings of Protestantism were ruthlessly and efficiently extinguished by an arm of state power – the Spanish Inquisition. Although what we might anachronistically term 'public opinion' was not a negligible factor (particularly in self-governing towns), state authorities made the decision whether or not to adopt the Reformation, and this, by definition, was a political calculation.

On what basis was that calculation made? The Reformation slips neatly, perhaps too neatly, into a broader narrative of European political change. That story can be called, in crude but allowable shorthand, the rise of the nation-state. Across Western and Central Europe in the later Middle Ages, secular rulers were consolidating and centralizing their authority, and interfering ever more directly in the running of the Church in their territories. The papal aspiration for universal spiritual monarchy, with the pontiff directly controlling the Church throughout Europe, and dictating terms to kings and emperors, peaked in the 12th century, and was more or less defunct by the beginning of the sixteenth. The popes of the Renaissance concerned themselves more modestly with the governance of the unruly papal states around Rome, and with the micro-politics of the Italian peninsula. Elsewhere, they settled for deference to their doctrinal authority, and for some negotiated involvement in the financial and managerial affairs of national churches. The repudiation of that residual power and influence is sometimes seen as part of a natural progression towards national autonomy and maturity on the part of European states. Yet the first regional rulers to show real enthusiasm for the Reformation were not the established national monarchs, but the wannabes: princelings who, under the nominal suzerainty of the emperor, governed German territories that were not quite kingdoms in scale or substance. The connection makes considerable sense. On the face of it, German princes had much to gain from adopting Luther's cause. Politically, they could consolidate ecclesiastical control in their territories, incorporating the church's administration into the mechanisms of government, while asserting greater freedom of manoeuvre *vis-à-vis* the emperor. Financially, they might with a (relatively) clear conscience plunder the wealth of the church, taxing the clergy and seizing the lands and endowments of monasteries. A case in point was Duke Ulrich, ruler of the southwestern territory of Württemberg, who confiscated three-quarters of all ecclesiastical property in the duchy, his agents scraping the gold paint from church altar-pieces. It is also true that – in contrast to a traditional Catholic insistence on the rights and liberties of the Church – Luther's theology could look remarkably ruler-friendly. As his 1525 outburst against rebelling peasants made clear, Luther was an instinctive proponent of political order, setting much store by St Paul's monition (Romans 13:1) that Christian souls should subject themselves to established authority, since 'the powers that be are ordained of God'. Luther was no fawning political sycophant: he regarded secular power as a kind of necessary evil, and in a 1523 treatise on *Temporal Authority: To What Extent it Should be Obeyed* memorably called princes 'usually the greatest fools or the worst knaves on earth', their function being to serve as 'God's jailers and hangmen'. The starting point of Luther's ecclesiology (doctrine of the Church) was that the 'true Church' was beyond all secular coercion and control, as it was an invisible union of the hearts and souls of justified Christians. But this left a messy morass of human wickedness to deal with in this world, which princes (ideally but not necessarily good ones) were tasked to contain and control. In what is sometimes called Luther's 'two kingdoms theory', the 'kingdom of God' was to be left to itself, but the 'kingdom of the world', including the outward forms of church organization, was a sphere of legitimate political compulsion. Luther thus approved Elector John's 'Visitation' of Saxony in 1528, which organized under princely auspices the introduction of Reformation into the rural parishes, and set up a territorial church as a branch of state administration.

Beyond a certain point, cynicism abut human motivation risks becoming a form of naivety. It is implausible that the rulers who steered their territories towards the Reformation all did so entirely on the basis of cold political calculation. For a start, there were considerable risks: the kings of England and Sweden both faced serious popular Catholic rebellions, and in the case of German princes, the wrath of the emperor was not to be taken lightly. For committed supporters of the Protestant cause such as Philip of Hesse or John Frederick of Saxony, it is likely that diplomatic and military expenditure in the 1530s and 1540s more than cancelled out profits from confiscated church revenues. John Frederick in particular proved his ideological mettle. Captured in 1547 at the crushing imperial victory at Mühlberg, he refused to recant his Protestantism or recognize the Augsburg Interim, accepting instead exile and imprisonment. By contrast, the most blatant case of religious policy driven by self-serving motives is probably that of Henry VIII, who discovered objections to papal authority in the early 1530s in order to fix his marital difficulties. But even Henry seems to have sincerely believed he was acting in accordance with God's will.

The politics of Reformation and Counter-Reformation were rarely clear-cut. For one thing, truths of faith aside, it was not obvious that opportunities for the enhancement of political and financial power were greater for rulers leaving the Catholic fold than for those remaining within it. The most powerful of Europe's national monarchs, the kings of France, drew immense kudos from the ceremonies and rituals of the Catholic Church, and from the title 'most Christian kings' which centuries earlier the papacy had bestowed on their line. There was in fact little, politically, to attract French monarchs to the Reformation, as under the terms of an agreement with the papacy in 1516 they enjoyed considerable rights to tax the clergy and control appointments within the French Catholic Church. It was much the same story in Spain, whose rulers had earned the papal title of 'Catholic Kings' for capturing the last Muslim stronghold of Granada in 1492. Other concessions included permission (1478) to set up and control a powerful ecclesiastical Inquisition, and the right, which turned out to be a very substantial one, to patronage over all ecclesiastical positions in the newly discovered territories of the Americas. Charles V and Philip II were undoubtedly sincerely pious, but their Catholicism did not impede their effectiveness as rulers. The threat of Protestantism could supply leverage for Catholic monarchs in their negotiations with the papacy. James V of Scotland, for example, was able to demand lucrative taxation rights over the Church as the price of his loyalty to Rome. The rulers of Bavaria, flag-bearers of beleaguered German Catholicism, were in the later 16th century granted extensive control over a virtually autonomous national Church, which the dukes administered through their own Clerical Council.

In the later 20th century we were urged to acknowledge 'the personal is the political'; in the later 16th century piety was political. When Duke Maximilian I of Bavaria (r. 1598–1651) ordered his subjects to carry a set of rosary beads around with them at all times, and to face fines or the pillory for eating meat on Fridays, he was making a statement about the kind of regime he headed, and the extent to which subjects must identify, in hearts and minds, with their ruler's priorities. There is a historians' term-of-art for the processes at work here. Since the 1970s, scholars have used 'confessionalization' to describe how the Reformation intersected with the agenda of state-building in an age of increasing political centralization. The argument is that political authorities across Europe in the later 16th and 17th centuries, Protestant and Catholic alike, assiduously promoted a single form of 'confessional' Christianity within their territories, and repressed alternatives, as a means of increasing control over their subjects. Confessional (from the Latin *confessio*, to acknowledge) here refers to the various confessions of faith, or statements of defined doctrine, which were drawn up as the religious divisions in Europe hardened and clarified from the mid-16th century. Members of the rival confessions were increasingly expected to identify culturally and politically with their church's teachings, and to know what those teachings were. Lutherans rallied around the Augsburg Confession of 1530 and the 1580 Book of Concord. The Reformed had the so-called Helvetic Confessions of 1536 and 1566, and the formulas of Calvinist orthodoxy from the 1619 Synod of Dort; Catholics, the decrees of Trent.

Counter-intuitively to our modern expectations, religion is here an agent of modernization, helping to create more uniform and obedient societies, suffused with a sense of patriotic and pious identification with the Lutheran, Calvinist, or Roman Catholic motherland. Only the Church had permanent representatives in every town and village, with the potential, via pulpit or confessional box, to reach the conscience of every subject. So control over religion, it has been argued, was more vital to the development of the modern state even than monopoly of military force, or a workable taxation system. Confessionalization was not an automatic process: it had to be worked at. Popular religious culture was often stubbornly local, regulated by tradition, and passive and undogmatic in outlook. Thus church and state authorities co-operated to bring people up to speed, requiring them to learn orthodox doctrine by attendance at sermons, Sunday schools, or catechism classes – all of which necessitated the active

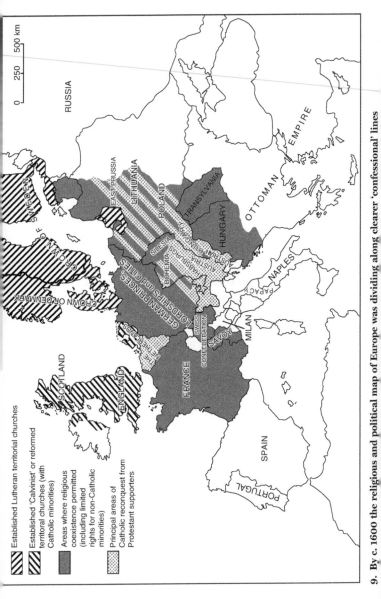

Established Lutheran territorial churches

Established 'Calvinist' or reformed territorial churches (with Catholic minorities)

Areas where religious coexistence permitted (including limited rights for non-Catholic minorities)

Principal areas of Catholic reconquest from Protestant supporters

9. By c. 1600 the religious and political map of Europe was dividing along clearer 'confessional' lines

67

participation of a reliable and properly educated body of clergy, with horizons beyond the boundaries of the village. The desired outcome was 'social discipline': having internalized their faith, Christians of varying stripes would become model subjects, less given to the riotous, licentious, or superstitious behaviour that caused concern to superiors.

One attraction of the 'confessionalization thesis' is that it gets us away from an old-fashioned doctrinally obsessed model of the Reformation, allowing us to view the process in more objective sociological terms, and to appreciate the extent to which Protestant and Catholic Reformations resembled each other, sharing objectives and methods. Yet this is also the theory's weakness, stressing religion's 'function' at the expense of its content, and ironing out the quirks and peculiarities that actually made religion meaningful for 16th- and 17th-century people. There is also the suspicion that one size doesn't really fit all. Confessionalization works well for certain German Protestant states, and outliers such as Sweden. It also looks plausible in 17th-century France, where Louis XIV's road to absolutism was paved with good Catholic intentions. But the designation is more awkward for other parts of the Catholic world, where the Church and its institutions maintained degrees of independence from the apparatus of the state. The reforming intentions of the Council of Trent – for example, over residence of bishops in their dioceses – were actually in conflict with priorities of Catholic rulers, who wished to continue to use bishoprics to reward their servants. And there are also important parts of Europe for which the confessionalization model doesn't seem to work at all, such as England and the Netherlands, which managed already in the 17th century to be religiously pluralistic without ceasing to be politically well-developed states. Undue concentration on 'state-building' in connection with the politics of the Reformation is also likely to obscure a phenomenon of great importance: the extent to which religious faith and fervour could be harmful to, or subversive of, the interests of sovereign rulers, and its potential to produce sustained and damaging conflict.

Wars of religion

The Reformation was an era of fairly unremitting ideological warfare in Europe, perhaps the first in which states fought each other for reasons other than territorial aggrandizement, or the honour and glory of their sovereigns. With the peculiar exception of crusades against infidels abroad, and (occasionally) heretics at home, medieval rulers did not really fight wars for religious reasons, for all that political and military alliances involving the pope were invariably christened 'Holy Leagues'. It would be difficult, if not impossible, to identify a 16th- or 17th-century conflict that was fought for *purely* religious reasons, uncontaminated by political, economic, or dynastic considerations. But religious rivalry produced conflicts within and between states that were more prolonged, bloody, and embittered than they would otherwise have been. The first identifiably religious war of the Reformation broke out in 1529, in a crucible of military energy and expertise, the Swiss Confederation, long-standing exporter of tough mercenary troops. Cooperation among the loose federation of autonomous cantons in Switzerland dissolved as some cantons adopted Protestantism, and others remained defiantly Catholic. In these circumstances, established arrangements for the joint administration of subject territories broke down, and war was declared. A renewed outbreak in 1531 led to the death of Huldrych Zwingli, probably the only front-rank theologian ever to lose his life in battle. Thereafter, one can compile a sorry litany of major armed conflicts with a sufficiently pronounced ideological element to be usefully termed religious wars: Charles V's conflicts with the German Protestant princes, 1547, and 1552–5; seven 'wars of religion' in France, 1562–98, with a sequel 1610–29; the protracted revolt of the Netherlands, 1567–1648; the Scottish civil wars of 1559–60 and 1567–73; Elizabethan England's war with Spain, 1585–1604; sporadic warfare and rebellion in Ireland, 1560–1603;

the Thirty Years War, 1618–48; civil wars in Britain and Ireland, 1637–54, and 1688–90; Louis XIV's repression of bloody Huguenot rebellion in 1702–11. War is always nasty, but ideological conflicts have a particular ability to produce atrocities. Dutch rebels targeted priests and friars in the 1570s, and Cromwell's soldiers slaughtered Catholic townspeople during the reconquest of Ireland in 1649. Perhaps the single most notorious incident – certainly in Protestant Europe, where memory of it was assiduously perpetuated – was the St Bartholomew's Day Massacre of 24 August 1572, which ushered in the fourth war of religion in France. During a period of tense and tenuous peace, a botched assassination attempt against the Huguenot leader Gaspard de Coligny inspired Charles IX and the powerful Queen Mother, Catherine de Medici, to pre-empt reprisals by finishing the job. Believing they had royal authority behind them, mobs of Catholics in Paris then turned on Huguenot neighbours in three days of savage slaughter, with a wave of massacres following in other towns across the country. At a minimum estimate, 2,000 men, women, and children were slain in Paris, and another 3,000 in the provinces. The violence was extreme, and frequently ritualistic: corpses were mutilated, pregnant women eviscerated. Heresy was perceived as a pollution, a plague, from which the city needed to be cleansed. Pope Gregory XIII saw the hand of God in the disaster which had befallen the Protestants, and ordered a commemorative medal to be struck.

Yet there was in the end to be no military solution to the problem of false belief. The religious wars seldom finished in total victory, and their endings required the combatants, literally, to come to terms with one another. The sporadic rounds of war and civil war left religious minorities entrenched in many European states: Catholics in the northern Netherlands, England, and Ireland (where they were numerically a majority); Protestants in France; Lutherans, Catholics, and Calvinists in various combinations in German states where another confession was dominant. The protection of minority co-religionists in officially hostile environments became a recognized aim of diplomacy: the treaties which ended the Thirty Years War would not have been accepted on any side without the rights of freedom of conscience and liberty for private worship they granted within the empire. There is a real irony here, for virtually no one regarded religious toleration as a positive good in itself. But if religious dissidents could not be eliminated, compromise was the price of peace, and toleration was an unforeseen outcome of war. Some old assumptions which the Reformations had emphatically sought to shore up – the fusion of religious and political loyalties, the complete identity of Christian culture and civil society – thus began slowly to unravel. When Catholics in Elizabethan or Stuart England protested their complete loyalty to the crown in 'civil' matters, they were implicitly proposing a separation of political and religious spheres, and demarcating a space where the authority of the state did not intrude.

Paths to resistance

If grudging official acceptance of religious minorities was a messy, pragmatic, and unexpected consequence of religious conflict, the Reformation also challenged the established status of political authority in more direct and self-conscious ways. The defiance of rulers by subjects of a different religious persuasion was a political fact on the ground, but the defiers wanted to feel legally and ethically justified in the steps they were taking. The result was another momentous development: an unprecedented theorizing of the limits of political obedience, and the articulation of fully fledged theories of subaltern resistance.

Of course, rebellion was not a new phenomenon in the 16th century, and rebels had always needed an excuse as well as a cause. The classic one was that insurgents were not really rebelling *against* the sovereign at all; they were acting to protect him from corrupt and wicked counsellors who had succeeded in leading him astray. This evasion still had legs in the Reformation era: it was the argument of the Yorkshire Catholic rebels who in 1536 rose against Henry VIII's policies in a 'Pilgrimage of Grace'. But as a basis for sustained ideological dissent, the argument was both implausible and impractical. Serious debates over the resistance question began in Lutheran Germany, as the Protestant princes considered options in the face of Charles V's hostility. Lutheran theologians produced an ingenious amalgam of doctrines of political obligation and constitutional theory. All rulers had an inescapable duty to protect and preserve true religion; at the same time, the German princes were jointly responsible with the emperor for the good order of the empire. If he failed in his duty to uphold true religion, acting as a tool of the anti-christian pope, then he could legitimately be resisted. This was not a recipe for anarchy, but a narrowly defined set of circumstances under which 'inferior magistrates' might call the superior magistrate to account.

Calvin's position was remarkably similar – he was not the revolutionary proponent of principled resistance he is sometimes cracked up to be. In the *Institutes* he observed merely that the constitutions of some states allowed for 'defenders of the people's freedom' to guard against tyranny – the ephors of ancient Sparta, or the tribunes of Rome. Cautiously, he added that the estates or parliaments of modern kingdoms 'perhaps' performed the same function. But Calvin's persistent diatribes against the horrors of 'false' worship, and the obligation on true Christians to shun it, were an invitation to at least passive resistance and civil disobedience. It was in response to actual persecutions, and the beginnings of Counter-Reformation in areas lacking the federated power structure of Germany, that some of Calvin's followers developed less equivocal and more radical arguments. A trio of refugees from Mary Tudor's England, Christopher Goodman, John Knox, and John Ponet, broke spectacularly from the notion that even ungodly rulers were (in the formula of St Paul) 'ordained of God', and concluded that wicked rulers could be overthrown or even killed – the doctrine of tyrannicide. Some French Calvinists went down the same path: Philippe du Plessis-Mornay's *Vindication Against Tyrants* (1579) argued that an ungodly monarch had forfeited the right to rule, having broken the terms of a covenant with God and the people, and similar conclusions were reached by the Scot George Buchanan. Principle was shortly put into practice in the Netherlands, where in 1580 the rebel leader William of Orange openly renounced the sovereignty of Philip II for having failed in his royal obligations. In the 17th century, the Protestant English deposed not one but two of their kings, Charles I and James II; the former for being insufficiently Protestant, and the latter for converting to Rome (some tender consciences hiding behind the fiction that James had 'abdicated' by fleeing the country).

Resistance theory was not a Protestant monopoly, and some of the most radical challenges to political authority were Catholic ones. The popes had long claimed a superior status to all secular monarchs, and the right, in extreme circumstances, to remove them from office. The papal 'deposing power' was pretty much a dead letter by the end of the Middle Ages, but the Reformation threatened to give it a new lease of life. A 1534 rebellion against Henry VIII in Ireland, led by the charismatic young earl of Kildare, marked a very early break with conventions of late medieval political protest. Kildare repudiated allegiance to Henry, and aspired to place Ireland under the direct sovereignty of the pope. A later, and equally unsuccessful Tudor rebellion – the 1569 Rising of the Northern Earls against Elizabeth I – encouraged Pius V to blow the dust off the deposing power. His bull *Regnans in Excelsis* of 1570 declared Elizabeth an excommunicated heretic, and ordered her subjects to withdraw obedience from her – a document making life very difficult for English Catholics over the following years. Subsequently, leading Jesuit theologians like the Italian Robert Belarmine, the Spaniard Francisco Suarez, and the Englishman Robert Persons developed justifications for tyrannicide that caught up with the Calvinist position. For Catholics as for Protestants, much of the momentum came from

10. A procession of the militant and anti-royalist French Catholic League in 1590, with prominent and heavily armed priests and friars

the situation in later 16th-century France, where the crown's move towards an increasingly 'politique' position infuriated the militant Catholic League, formed to resist political compromise with the Huguenots.

After Henry III ordered the assassination of the League leader, the duke of Guise, in 1588, preachers openly called for his overthrow as a tyrant. The practice, as well as theory of tyrannicide became something of a Catholic speciality in these years. The first modern-style assassination of a head of state was the shooting by a French Catholic of William of Orange, in Delft in 1584. Henry III and Henry IV of France were both stabbed to death by fanatical Catholics, in 1589 and 1610. And James I of England narrowly escaped a still more spectacular end in 1605, when papist conspirators plotted to blow up parliament with a huge quantity of gunpowder.

After the upheavals of the wars of religion subsided, the immediate outcome of the Reformation was probably to enhance and entrench political authority. With a few notable exceptions (such as England and the Netherlands), 'absolutism' was the order of the day for later 17th-century European states, with representative assemblies in decline and the untrammelled exercise of monarchical power presented as a positive good. Resistance theories went out of fashion, as the product of a violent and divisive recent past. But the formulation of considered justifications of political non-compliance, based on a contractual element in the three-way relationship between ruler, ruled, and God, was of considerable significance for the future. Their originators aimed not, of course, at the establishment of democracy, or political liberty for its own sake, but at the extirpation of 'idolatry' and 'heresy'. Nonetheless, these works would exert influence on the revolutionaries of the 18th century, American and French, and thus play a part in the inauguration of a new and very different political world.

Chapter 4
Society

In October 1987, Prime Minister Margaret Thatcher told readers of a women's magazine that 'you know, there is no such thing as society. There are individual men and women, and there are families.' Thatcher was the daughter of a Methodist lay preacher, and thus a spiritual great-granddaughter of the Reformation. Although the stark and self-reliant individualism encapsulated in her philosophy is often supposed to be a cultural off-shoot of Protestantism, her blunt aphorism would have made little sense to any 16th- or 17th-century reformer, Protestant or Catholic. From their perspective, human beings were fundamentally defined by their relationships to others, and by their place in social structures of various kinds. The Reformation was a collective enterprise geared, not just to the saving of individual souls, but to the transformation of the entire *societas christianorum*, the fraternity of Christians. It is a truism to observe that the titles of books and articles addressing themselves to 'Religion and Society' in the medieval or Reformation periods actually set up an unreal dichotomy: what we would today class as 'religion' was so woven into the fabric of social organization and day-to-day living that attempts to extract it risk falsifying the lived experience of our ancestors. It follows that the Reformation, in seeking to alter the language, symbols, and rituals of communal Christianity, changed relationships with neighbours and the very textures of everyday life. At the same time, those textures and relationships shaped the Reformation, which was not just something imposed on society, but itself a deeply social phenomenon.

Structures of community

Investment in 'community' was not a lifestyle choice for pre-modern people, but a necessity of existence. Agriculture (the occupation of the great majority of the population) was a fundamentally collective exercise, in which all planted and ploughed according to agreed conventions, and brought in the harvest together. If the sustaining of life was a collective business, so were the principal threats to it: harvest failure, epidemic disease, extreme weather, war. These were often seen, in a phrase still embedded in the small print of insurance policies, as 'acts of God'. The Lord might reward or punish individuals, but his judgements might also be felt by communities as a whole. This made everybody's behaviour everybody's business: all would suffer if the immorality, or heresy, of a few brought down God's wrath upon the society tolerating them. Towns, cradles of modern individualism and anomie, were in the 16th century just as communally and collectively minded as the countryside, seeing themselves as sacred communities with a responsibility for the moral wellbeing of all their inhabitants, something which may explain why the theologies of Zwingli and Martin Bucer, imbued with the spirit of civic humanism, appealed more to townspeople than those of the solitary monk, Martin Luther. Early modern people depended heavily on each other, as husbands, wives, children, masters, apprentices, neighbours, guild members, and fellow-parishioners. It would not be surprising if they hoped they might get to heaven together too.

Here again, we see the strokes of the Reformation running along, rather than cutting against, the grain of late medieval religious culture. The principal block of both religious and social organization was the parish, a local administrative unit to which all who lived within its boundaries by definition belonged. The parish church was typically 'community centre' as well as place of worship, the only substantial collectively owned building and the site of communal festivity. Parishioners supported their local priest through the payment of tithes, a tax of 10% on all income and agricultural produce. In return, the priest was expected to supply pastoral care, and the sacraments, from baptism to extreme unction, which were essential keys to the doorway of salvation. Ensuring a reliable quantity and quality of such services was an understandable preoccupation of village life. Already before the Reformation a number of Swiss and German communities were securing property and endowments to hire and control their own priests. In the early years of reform, leading up to and culminating in the Peasants' War, many local communities sifted from the reformers' messages a pledge of improved and simplified pastoral care, of greater clerical accountability, and of more secure collective salvation.

Even if expectations were to be disappointed, there were continuities to appreciate. Where Protestantism became the established faith, it retained the existing parish system, and made community cohesion, oversight, and control central features of its pastoral mission. Only in this context can we understand the passions raised by the matter of excommunication, whether issued by Catholic church courts or Genevan consistories. Excommunication was not merely a source of social disgrace (at least for more respectable members of the community), it was also an exclusion from crucial participation in community life, principally the sacrament of communion that symbolized one's status and good standing among neighbours. Nor could excommunicates, barred from acting as godparents, play any part in the sacrament of baptism. Godparenthood, unlike its pale shadow today, was a vital social institution, providing a child with a lifelong patron, and creating bonds of spiritual kinship between families. Calvinist reformers were suspicious of the institution, suspecting a potential for superstition, but Calvin was not able to eliminate it from the Genevan baptismal ceremony any more than Puritans were able to abolish it in 17th-century England.

Perhaps the test of any community is how it treats marginal and disadvantaged members. Christ had warned that 'the poor are with you always', but the Reformation was a pivotal moment for redefining their relationship to the rest of the community and formulating practical solutions for their relief. Poverty as a concept, and the poor as participants in a drama of salvation, played important roles in medieval Catholic culture. Poverty was holy, the estate of the apostles, and though the poor suffered in this life, they were especially beloved of Christ and rewarded in the next. The Church had its own institutionalized poverty, in the persons of the begging or mendicant friars, whose sermons castigated the rich for lack of charity. 'Charity' meant, not as today, mere altruism towards the unfortunate, but a state of right social relations, which restored all the partners to God's favour. Giving alms to the poor was a charitable deed, a good work contributing to the donor's eventual salvation. The poor for their part had the charitable obligation to pray for their benefactors' welfare, in this life and the next.

For Protestant reformers, giving to the poor was not a 'good work', there was no spiritual exchange of benefits, and no sense in which the poor particularly resembled Christ. Nonetheless, Protestant propaganda tended to castigate Catholics not for doing too much for the poor, but too little. The money spent on adorning shrines and images of saints, on lighting candles or paying priests to pray for the dead; all this could more profitably go towards the relief of the poor. The 16th century was an era of great social and economic dislocation, of population pressure on resources and rising inflation. Conventional wisdom credits the Protestant Reformation with getting serious about poverty, ceasing to romanticize it, and setting up properly prioritized schemes for the support of the 'deserving poor'. In fact, older forms of indiscriminate and sporadic charity were starting to change in some places before the Reformation. The Catholic Spanish humanist Juan Luis Vives (1492–1540) advocated that town magistrates, rather than the Church, should assume responsibility for poor relief, consolidating private and parochial funds to sustain those unable to work, while 'sturdy' beggars should be banished or made to labour. Ideas of this sort, placing restrictions on begging, were put into practice in London in 1514–18, and more comprehensively in Ypres in 1531. Starting with Luther's Wittenberg, many Protestant towns put similar schemes into effect, prohibiting begging, mandating regular collections for the establishment of a 'common chest' to support the poor, and sometimes establishing civic workhouses. Private donations to the poor did not cease, and the Protestant churches (particularly Calvinist ones) often retained parallel systems of charity, just as municipal systems of poor relief multiplied across the towns of Catholic Europe. But Protestantism more emphatically moved primary responsibility for the problem of poverty from the Church to the state, and understood it as part of the enforcement of public order. This did not necessarily 'secularize' the issue in our sense of the term. Protestant poor relief was underpinned by 'correct' doctrine, and was part of building a genuinely Christian community. It was also accompanied by attempts to regulate, control, and reform the moral behaviour of the poor, requiring them to demonstrate a pious demeanour as a condition of support. In areas where two confessions existed side by side, it could also become an instrument of religious discipline and confessional cohesion. Church communities gave to 'their' poor, and charity became exclusive, a mark of belonging.

Success in building a godly community depended on one social group above all others: the clergy. The Catholic clergy were at the sharp end of the Reformation's attack on traditional religious practice. Reformers rejected the idea of a separate clerical caste or estate, marked off by legal privileges, ritual celibacy, and such outward status markers as a shaved or 'tonsured' head. Priests were no longer the special channels of God's grace through their unique ability to perform the miracle of the mass; Luther taught that 'we are all equally priests' through baptism, with clergy duties being no more than a function delegated to some members of the community. In its first phases, the Reformation was intensely, virulently, anticlerical, its propaganda prints depicting friars and monks as, literally, the defecations of the devil. A man seeing a priest in a Cambridgeshire village in the 1520s, 'took up a cow turd with his spade, and clapped it upon his crown', saying 'all the sort of you will ere it be long be glad to hide your shaven pates'. Some asked whether a distinct clerical profession was necessary at all, if salvation came through faith, and the vernacular Word of God in scripture. Most anticlerical of all were the anabaptists, who believed simple folk were quite capable of assimilating the messages of the bible on their own, without the intervention of bookish pastors.

It is characteristic of revolutions to have to rebuild what they have earlier torn down. Both secular and church authorities across the Lutheran and Reformed worlds soon realized that well-heeled and respected clergymen were vital instruments of religious instruction for the laity, and key agents of social discipline. The Protestant minister may not have possessed the mystique of the mass, or the charisma of the confessional, but he was expected to wield moral and religious authority in the community he served, principally in his role as preacher of the Word (Reformed pastors tended to sport full beards, like Old Testament prophets). By the early 17th century, Protestant clergy in most places were likely to be university-educated, and were acquiring the status and characteristics of a 'profession'. There were, in fact, more similarities than they would have cared to recognize with the parish priests of the Catholic Reformation, who, as the seminary system started to bed down, were similarly more learned than their predecessors. In both cases, education may have been a mixed blessing: clergy were better able to articulate the doctrines of their respective churches, but they were apt to be 'outsiders' in the communities they served, more culturally distant from the day-to-day concerns of parishioners than the humble local boys who typically served as medieval parish priests. Protestant and Catholic pastors could be equally touchy about their rights and status, and anticlericalism continued to be a low-key but persistent feature of different church settings, with the potential to burn bright in times of tumult or crisis.

A key difference between Protestant and Catholic clergy, however, was their permitted relationship to sex. Trent maintained the discipline of celibacy for the priesthood, and in practice the bishops of the Catholic Reformation considerably tightened it up, though scandals were never eliminated. For Protestants, by contrast, the most palpable pointer to the priesthood of all believers was that ministers were allowed, even encouraged, to get married. Luther himself led the way here in 1525, taking as his bride – to the revulsion of Catholic Europe – an ex-nun, Katharina von Bora. It was a symbol of Protestantism's impulse to redeem and reform, and also to control, the most basic components of human society.

Sexuality, women, and family

Catholicism's retention of clerical celibacy endorsed the longstanding view that, although marriage was a sacrament, and a holy ordinance of God, complete abstinence from sex was the more spiritually perfect state. Virginity had some heavy-weight role-models: St John, St Paul, Mary Mother of God, Christ himself. Medieval monks and nuns (in theory) resembled the angels in their chastity. Protestantism's pessimistic view of mankind encouraged the perception that professed chastity, other than for an exceptional few, was bound to be hypocrisy. Sexuality – a consequence of Adam and Eve's Fall – needed a legitimate outlet, and the only such outlet was marriage. A feature of the Lutheran Reformation in German cities was an attack on the public brothels, maintained by civic authorities as an acceptable channel for the sexual energies of unruly youth, and even tacitly accepted by pre-Reformation clerics as a necessary evil, a sewer maintaining the moral hygiene of wider society. But for reformers, the only acceptable sexual acts were procreative ones between husband and wife. 'Sodomy' remained a heinous moral offence, as well as a capital crime, in both Protestant and Catholic societies throughout the Reformation period.

Although removing its sacramental status, reformers raised the status of marriage by eliminating the competition: monastic life no longer existed as a spiritually superior alternative. Married life and Christian life were now effectively the same thing for adults. As the most fundamental religious and social institution of society, marriage required close regulation. Medieval canon law and sacramental theology held that a marriage was a contract (requiring free consent) between two partners, who were themselves the ministers of the sacrament. The public declaration of marriage banns, a blessing in church, the participation of a priest, and the consent of parents were all desirable, but not essential to a marriage's validity. Among wealthy families, the phenomenon of youthful elopement – 'clandestine marriage' – was a persistent source of grievance. The Reformation moved to police marriage more closely as a component of an ordered society. In both Lutheran and Reformed territories, parents were given the right of veto over children's marriages, and the blessing of a minister became mandatory. Similar social concerns motivated the Fathers of Trent, who in 1563 declared a church ceremony and the presence of witnesses (though not necessarily the consent of parents) to be necessary components of a valid marriage. For Catholics, the sacramental status of marriage made (and still makes) it an indissoluble lifelong bond. But for Protestants, the dissolution of marriages became imaginable. Luther thought it permissible in cases of adultery, impotence, or refusal of conjugal rights; Zwingli added abandonment to the list. With the demise of the old episcopal courts, new marriage courts regulated divorce, which in practice was extremely rare in Protestant Europe. Reformed England kept its medieval church courts, but by a quirk of history never introduced divorce legislation, and up until the mid-19th century, private acts of parliament were the only means to secure a full divorce.

The family was the Protestant social institution par excellence, the building-block of the Christian community, and at the same time a portrait in miniature of how that society was to be structured. In Calvin's view, the household resembled a private church, in which father played the role of minister, disciplining and instructing the domestic congregation of wife, children, and servants.

The Reformation was an era when fathers ruled. Its basic presumptions about family and domestic life are aptly described as patriarchal. The implications of this for the experience of childhood were probably mixed. Children were regarded, like the rest of humanity, as intrinsically bad, rather than naturally innocent. They were to be ruled by the rod, restrained and restricted, and indoctrinated (in a morally neutral sense of that term) with the messages of the catechism. But just as the Old

11. Anthonius Claessins's painting (c. 1585) of a family saying grace before a meal presents an idealized picture of godly domestic order

Testament commanded the honouring of parents, the New instructed fathers to 'provoke not your children to anger'. Children were gifts of God, and reformers taught that they should be nurtured and cared for. One theory holds that the punitive mortality rates of early modern Europe (half of all children died before their tenth birthday) discouraged parents from making any real emotional investment in their offspring. Yet a wealth of surviving evidence suggests otherwise: Luther himself was distraught upon the death of his daughter Magdalene in 1542.

If the Reformation reinforced patriarchy, did it therefore diminish the status of women? There are arguments both for and against this view, though the notion that women, in this period or any other, constitute a unitary block with common interests and aspirations is a questionable one. It is often suggested that in elevating the standing of marriage, reformers raised the dignity of women, though a positive view of marriage and a positive view of women are not necessarily identical. The Reformation did little to change existing stereotypes that women were unruly and sexually voracious. Unmarried (and therefore masterless) women might be regarded as dangerous, and laws in various places prohibited them from taking up residence in cities, or living on their own. Within marriage, contemporary attitudes could be bruising to modern sentiments. 'Reasonable' physical chastisement of wives by husbands was a social norm, and in a notorious passage Luther remarked that 'if women grow weary or even die while bearing children, that does no harm. Let them bear children to death, that's what they're there for.' Yet Luther's own union, like many Protestant marriages, was an affectionate and companionable one.

In terms of Christian vocation or calling, the Protestant Reformation offered women only the dual package of marriage and motherhood. It removed the distinctive religious path open to women in the Middle Ages, as sisters under vows in convents. Not all nuns, of course, had sincere religious vocations. Many had entered religious life as young girls, and some (such as Katharina von Bora) were happy to leave when opportunity presented. But the idea that the Reformation 'liberated' women from the corrupt and stultifying confines of the cloister now seems a rather Victorian one. Along with all-female confraternities (also abolished by the reformers), convents represented a rare opportunity for women to express themselves spiritually and creatively in their own social space, and for this reason have started to attract the admiring attention of modern feminist scholars. In German towns, some of the most effective resistance to the onset of the Reformation came from nuns. The humanist abbess of the Franciscan Poor Clares in Nuremberg, Caritas Pirckheimer, simply refused to leave, withstanding with her sisters a barrage of Protestant sermons, and skirmishing vigorously with the city council until her death in 1532. In a number of places in Germany, in fact, the authorities decided it was simpler to let convents gradually die out, leaving them alone, but refusing to let them take new novices. The approach was more brutal in Henry VIII's England, where all nunneries were closed in the later 1530s by royal command. Here, the usual Reformation prescription for the welfare of ex-nuns, supplying them with dowries towards their marriage, was ruled out, Henry perversely insisting that monastic vows of celibacy were binding even after monasticism ceased to exist.

The demise of female monasticism in the Protestant world was paralleled by a spectacular renaissance in the Catholic one. Over the course of the 17th century, women came to form an absolute majority of persons in religious life. Some Catholic centres were awash with nuns, most notably Venice, where about half of all women from the wealthy governing class entered convents around the turn of the 17th century. They led cultured and not very ascetic lives there, preserving family estates from the erosion of multiple dowries. But the expansion of women religious was undoubtedly part of the explosion of religious energy in the Catholic Reformation more generally, as well as an assertion by women of their distinctive spirituality. New women's orders were founded, often with an innovative 'activist' bent. The Ursulines established in the 1530s by the Italian Angela Merici, and the French Visitandines, founded two generations later by Jeanne-Françoise de Chantal and Francis de Sales, had a remit of caring for the poor and sick. But the idea of women performing a public religious ministry increasingly caused unease to the Roman authorities. Separate attempts by the Spaniard Isabel Roser and the Englishwoman Mary Ward to establish female branches of the Jesuit Order were blocked by the papacy, which also in the 17th century insisted upon stricter 'enclosure' of Visitandines and Ursulines. Nonetheless, by insisting on a status as lay 'congregations', without habits or vows, some communities of women were able to continue charitable work in wider society, such as the Daughters of Charity founded by Vincent de Paul and Louise de Marillac in 1633. And even from behind convent walls, women could make remarkable contributions to the religious culture of the age: the writings of the Spanish Carmelite Teresa of Avila (1515–82) stand alongside the *Spiritual Exercises* of Loyola as some of the greatest Catholic devotional works.

Too often, scholarship focuses upon the Reformation's impact upon women, rather than women's impact on the Reformation. Women were not supposed to participate actively in the religious changes of the era, but many did, displaying fervent, even fanatical, partisan commitments. A remarkably high percentage (51 out of 280-odd) of the Protestants burned by Mary Tudor's regime were female. Under the Protestant government of Elizabeth I, women played a crucial role in the preservation of English Catholicism, exploiting the fact that wives had no separate legal identity from their husbands, and could not be fined for 'recusancy' so long as their husbands attended church. Female activism seems particularly pronounced in the developing world of 'voluntary' religion: in the late 17th-century Lutheran renewal movement known as pietism, in anabaptist groups like the Dutch Mennonites, and in the sects of interregnum England, the Baptists and Quakers,

12. This engraving, after Egbert van Heemskerk, shows a woman preaching at an English Quaker meeting – a shocking occurrence to respectable 17th-century opinion

where membership lists show women outnumbering men two-to-one.

New religious movements may have offered more scope for expression, and to achieve positions of influence. But women were often the most committed and devout members of established churches as well. A pronounced feature of modern Western culture – the feminization of religion – was firmly underway in a patriarchal age.

Culture wars?

A chapter on the reformation of society invites the question of whether society wanted to be reformed. In many ways, it didn't.

Clerical reformers, Protestant and Catholic, wanted better-educated, more devout, and less 'superstitious' congregations. Where local customs and rituals were an obstacle to these objectives, they sought to abolish them. Both Protestant and Catholic authorities in Germany, for example, tried hard to suppress suggestive fertility customs, such as young men harnessing local girls to ploughs on Ash Wednesday. They also discouraged the lighting of bonfires on the midsummer festival dedicated, since the coming of Christianity, to St John the Baptist. But villagers were attached to such traditions, and suspicious of innovation. Perhaps there was a fundamental non-meeting of minds. University-educated pastors understood religion as a force for moral renewal, a training course for heaven; illiterate rural folk, it is sometimes suggested, regarded it as a practical reservoir of magic to draw on for help with the day-to-day problems of disease, crop failure, and sick livestock. Among the laity, approved Protestant piety may have appealed disproportionately to local elites; respectable, literate people who could appreciate learned sermons and vernacular bibles, and who had a vested interest in curbing the disorderly conduct of their poorer neighbours.

Anyone anxious to suggest that at a popular level the Protestant and Catholic Reformations 'failed' has little difficulty amassing evidence in support of the case. Clerical complaints about the ignorance, immorality, and superstition of country folk abound, from Lutheran Germany as well Catholic France. They were just as common in Reformed territories, from Scotland to Switzerland, where consistory supervision should have meant social discipline was intense and effective. In the Pays de Vaud, for example, there were recurrent complaints in the mid-17th century of local people venerating a sacred tree trunk, which they believed had the power of healing gout. In 1662, a full century after the Council of Trent, the Catholic archbishop of Cologne was complaining about people's faith in astrological predictions, interpretation of dreams, and magical use of amulets and relics. Jesuits in Italy and Spain

13. Hans Sebald Beham's depiction (1520) of a raucous and ribald popular festival, *The Dance of the Noses*, exemplifies the kinds of activities reformers were keen to suppress

called the rural hinterlands to which they went on mission their 'Indies', because of the ignorance and uncouthness of the populace.

But to view the processes of Reformation as a head-on collision between 'elite' and 'popular' culture is too simplistic. For a start, although it is currently fashionable to stress the parallels and similarities of Catholic and Protestant reform, there were some crucial differences. Catholic reformers wanted a purified, more disciplined and clerically controlled Catholicism, but, unlike their Protestant counterparts, they had no desire to repudiate the existing religious culture of the people or many of its underlying presumptions. Concern for souls in purgatory, belief in miracles, the cult of the saints – these were common ground on which Catholic reformers could build. Festivals and processions to honour patron saints were fine, if supervised by the clergy, and unaccompanied by dissipation. Confraternities were a potential problem, if dominated by lay people, and threatening to become a rival source of loyalty to the parish. But reformers actively encouraged the formation of new 'rosary confraternities', which promoted through recital of the rosary devotion a disciplined, interiorized piety in tune with clerical priorities. Traditional and local saints' cults were supplemented in the 17th century by encouragement of devotion to new, universally venerated saints, some of whom were recent heroes of the Counter-Reformation: Ignatius Loyola, Francis Xavier, Carlo Borromeo. Catholic missioners, particularly Jesuits, understood what people wanted from the saints and were sometimes prepared to meet them more than half way, for example distributing 'Xavier water' which had been blessed by contact with a relic or medal of St Francis Xavier. Peasants in the Eifel in the early 18th century sprinkled it on their fields to eliminate a plague of caterpillars. But it was probably never true that such 'magical' use of divine power was the sum and substance of popular religious mentalities. In their own way, people grasped the Church's teachings about right living and salvation, and were open to some of what Catholic reformers had to say. If jargon words are required, 'negotiation' and 'accommodation' seem the appropriate ones here.

It was harder for Protestant reformers to bridge the gap between message and audience, but they were sometimes surprisingly prepared to have a go. Lutheran ministers in Denmark were willing to continue the ritual blessing of fields around Easter time, and in the Gaelic-speaking highlands of Scotland, Calvinist ministers had a liturgy for the blessing of fishermen's boats. Ethnic hostilities prevented similar accommodations to the culture of the people in Ireland, which must be a reason why the Reformation failed to take root there. Elsewhere, Protestantism generated recognizably confessional but genuinely popular forms of religious culture. In 17th-century England, annual commemorations of the 1605 Gunpowder Plot helped fuse anti-Catholic and nationalist sentiments. Numerous stories circulated in 17th- and 18th-century

Chapter 5
Culture

The 20th century's greatest Protestant theologian, Karl Barth, was of the view that no human art should attempt to portray the person of Jesus Christ. Endeavours to do so constituted a 'sorry story', and he urged Christian artists, however talented, to 'give up this unholy undertaking'. Barth stood at the end of a long line in Protestant, specifically Calvinist, thinking which held that art and religion, like oil and water, couldn't and shouldn't mix. Attempts to represent the divine, to capture anything of the ultimate majesty of God in merely human creativity, were at best pointless, at worst profoundly dangerous. The Protestant Reformation is widely credited with having 'secularized' art; if true, an impressive but ambiguous achievement. In some people's opinions, this served to rob art of its transcendent power, its ability to say anything ultimately meaningful about the universe, reducing it to mere aestheticism. Others suppose that it liberated art from dogmatic shackles, enabling it to explore all facets of human experience more fully and creatively. Protestantism's relationship with the arts, 'culture' in our modern sense, was by no means a straightforward one: the Reformation was never simply an anti-cultural force. Protestants understood the power of visual imagery. Paradoxically, Barth kept above his desk, and often meditated upon, a copy of one of the most emotive of 15th-century crucifixion scenes, the Isenheim altarpiece of Matthias Grünewald.

And the Reformation's appreciation for cultural media beyond painting and sculpture is constitutive of its identity and achievement. The other painting hanging in Barth's study (apart from one of Calvin) was a portrait of Mozart.

Visual culture

Pre-Reformation religion was intensely sensual, engaging the full range of worshippers' senses, but its visual aspects stand out. From great cathedrals to humble chapels, churches were filled with imagery: painted altarpieces, frescoed walls, elaborate statues of the Virgin and other saints. Great carvings of Christ upon the cross (in England called 'roods') dominated the sight-lines of churches from their position atop the roodscreen dividing the altar space from main congregational area. The classic defence of religious images was that they were didactic aids for the illiterate, 'laymen's books'. But the lovingly carved, painted, and gilded images of saints, which lay people paid for and then venerated with offerings and lighted candles, were more than just pictorial text. Images were prisms of sacral power, sites where the attentive presence of the saint was most likely to be focused and prayers most likely to be answered. Nor were images purely passive objects of perception: under the 'intromission' theory of vision prevalent in the late medieval and early modern periods, objects emitted ray-like descriptions of themselves for the eyes to receive and the faculties to reconstitute. Images acted upon the percipient, and were thus immensely potent.

Many images and paintings were no doubt aesthetically crude, but the century preceding Luther's protest witnessed an unprecedented outpouring of exquisite artistic expression in Europe. Catholic religious images of immense beauty and affective power were produced by painters like van Eyck and van der Weyden in the Netherlands, Lochner and Grünewald in Germany, and outstanding talents too numerous to begin listing in *quattrocento* Italy. Such painters and their workshops undertook 'secular' commissions, portraits of aristocrats and wealthy burghers, but their greatest works were devotional ones, and the Church was the pre-eminent patron of artistic production. The Reformation of the 16th century repudiated this extraordinary inheritance, and destroyed much of it, not out of philistinism or lack of appreciation for the power of art, but out of a heightened sensitivity to it, and an intense fear of the dangers of idolatry. 'Iconoclasm' – the destruction of religious images for overtly ideological reasons – may be the Reformation's most tangible bequest to the variegated cultural environments of modern Europe. Some areas – the Iberian peninsula, Italy – were relatively untouched; others experienced an artistic holocaust. Very little remains, for example, of the religious art of late medieval Scotland, and the tally for England is scarcely better: from around 9,000 medieval parish churches that possessed one, not a single undamaged rood remains today.

Attitudes varied among leading reformers to the risks and potential of religious imagery. A decisive moment for the cultural development of Lutheran Reform was Luther's decision, on his return to Wittenberg in 1522, to halt the iconoclasm initiated by his headstrong colleague Karlstadt. Luther, perhaps because he himself was not particularly moved by the power of painting or sculpture, considered images 'neither good nor bad' – they were in themselves, in a theological category developed by Melanchthon, examples of 'adiaphora', indifferent things which the Church could retain or abandon without moral hazard. What mattered was how they were used: worshipping of images, or constructing them in the hope of acquiring merit in God's eyes, was an abomination, but as means of instruction for the 'weak' they were acceptable. Thus precious Gothic art works survived in the churches of Lutheran Nuremberg, as more humble altarpieces and crucifixes have done in the parish churches of Lutheran Scandinavia. Lutheranism also generated its own religious artworks, through winning the allegiance of significant artists. Albrecht Dürer became Luther's disciple too late in life to produce recognizably 'Reformation' art, but the movement acquired a prize cultural asset in Lucas Cranach the elder (1472–1553), already in situ in Witttenberg as court painter to Frederick the Wise. In addition to a series of iconic portraits of Luther himself, Cranach provided illustrations for Luther's New Testament, as well as vivid sets of paired images to accompany the *Passional Christi und Antichristi* – a text contrasting the worldly and anti-Christian pope with the humble devotion of Christ to the poor. Cranach's paintings and altarpieces for Lutheran churches were heavily didactic allegorizations of key salvation themes: the dialectic of Law and Gospel, the redemptive blood of Jesus flowing without any earthly mediator.

Lutheranism's openness, within limits, to the religious utility of visual imagery was not shared by leaders of the Reformed tradition. Zwingli was a self-confessed connoisseur – 'pretty pictures and statues as such give me much pleasure' – but he was emphatic they had no place in churches or part to play in worship. Allowing them such a role was to usurp and misdirect honour due to God alone, and to insult God's invisible majesty by putting trust in created things. The divergent paths followed by Luther and Zwingli reflected different readings of the scriptural signposts. The fundamental and normative basis of divine law was the Ten Commandments, revealed by God to Moses, and recorded in the Old Testament books of Exodus and Deuteronomy. These began by instructing people to 'have no other Gods before me' and went on to prohibit the making of 'graven images' and bowing down to or serving them. But was this one commandment or two? The texts supplied more than ten injunctions, and gave no explicit guidance on how they were to be grouped. Jewish tradition held that the prohibition on graven imagery was a separate second commandment, while St Augustine's interpretation that it was simply a gloss on the first was authoritative for the medieval Catholic West. If that was so, then the ban logically applied to idols of false gods, not to all religious imagery. Luther stuck with Augustine, with the result that to this day Lutherans, along with

Catholics, number the commandments differently from other Protestants, including Anglicans. (Orthodox Christianity had never adopted the Augustinian numbering, which is why the abundant religious imagery of Eastern churches solely comprises two-dimensional icons, i.e. not 'graven'.) For Zwingli, as for Calvin, however, there was an explicit scriptural proscription against attempts to represent the divine. According to Calvin, 'since God has no similarity to those shapes by means of which people attempt to represent him, then all attempts to depict him are an impudent affront... to his majesty and glory'. Images were by definition idols, props of false worship, and a contagion and pollution to be eliminated from any Christian commonwealth.

Ideally, this was a tidy and state-sanctioned process. In Zürich, workmen and officials went into all the churches at midsummer 1524, locked the doors, and spent nearly two weeks dismantling the accumulated material piety of generations of townsfolk. The churches became white-washed halls for the hearing of sermons. In Tudor England successive waves of iconoclasm were carried out in orderly fashion by parish churchwardens, responding, perhaps grudgingly, to government orders. But in other places iconoclasm was the radical and democratic face of Protestant activism, unofficial, and designed to force the pace of magisterial change. Popular iconoclasm could also take highly ritualized forms, becoming a specialized rite of violence designed to demonstrate the 'powerlessness' of the image and of the belief system it represented. (One of Luther's objections was that he worried the destruction of images might itself take on the character of a ritual 'good work'.) Iconoclasts in Basel shouted out 'if you are God defend yourself, if you are human bleed!', as they threw onto the fire the crucifix from the city's Great Minster in 1529. Elsewhere images of saints were humiliated by being smeared with blood or filth, thrown into rivers or down latrines, or undergoing 'capital punishment' in staged mock executions. In Dundee in 1537, two men were wanted by the authorities for showing what they thought of the friars by 'hanging of the image of St Francis'. The largest waves of popular iconoclasm accompanied Calvinist revolt against established Catholic authority at the turn of the 1560s. A fiery sermon by John Knox stirred zealots in the university and cathedral town of St Andrews to descend on the churches so that, in a chronicler's words, 'before the sun was down, there was never inch standing but bare walls'. French cities saw bouts of violent and destructive iconoclasm in 1559–62, a major factor in the polarization preceding religious civil war. And at the start of the Dutch Revolt, an 'iconoclastic fury' swept across the Netherlands, with over 400 churches sacked in 1566 in Flanders alone. The destruction of images was an uncompromising statement which widened existing divisions, and not just between Catholic and Protestant. Iconoclastic incidents during the Calvinist 'Second Reformation' in Germany provoked reactive riots by Lutheran mobs, while Protestant image-breaking in the Baltic region deeply antagonized the neighbouring Eastern Orthodox, a group with whom reformers might have hoped to make common cause. The status of 'idols' was a neuralgic point in the divisions among English Protestants in the 1630s, and the outbreak of Civil War was the signal for a renewed campaign to 'purify' parish churches.

It seems unlikely that either destroyers or defenders of images were much motivated by what we might consider aesthetic considerations – few in the period would have understood what John Keats was on about in proposing that 'beauty is truth, truth beauty'. The truth, not the beauty, of religious art was precisely the point at issue. Ironically, it is likely that the largest-scale Christian iconoclasm of the mid-16th century was carried out not by Calvinists, but by Catholics, purging the newly acquired territories of Mexico and Peru of the symbols of pagan religion. The Franciscan archbishop of Mexico, Juan de Zumárraga, boasted in 1531 that he had presided over the destruction of 500 temples and 26,000 idols.

But the threat to old images in Europe may have prompted some to reflect on their artistic worth. Probably the most important rescue

Incendio de todas las ropas y libros y atavios de los sacerdotes ydolatricos
que se los quemaron los frayles

14. Franciscan friars put pagan 'idols' to the flames in 16th-century Mexico, a reminder that not all iconoclasts were Protestants

of an artwork in this period was the action of the town authorities of Ghent in spiriting away from iconoclasts in 1566 Van Eyck's extraordinary altarpiece, 'the adoration of the mystic lamb'. Whether the magistrates were motivated by civic pride, or by a sense of cultural value, art-lovers owe them a debt.

Protestantism's rejection of the salvific value of religious imagery prompted the Catholic Reformation to reassert it, and to explore new ways for art to connect worshippers to the divine. The Council of Trent, in a decree on the veneration of saints and the role of images, confirmed that 'great profit is derived from all sacred images', which taught lay people about the benefits of Christ and the miracles of the saints. But it injected a strong note of restraint, insisting on decorousness, pictorial clarity, doctrinal relevance, and the avoidance of figure painting 'with a beauty exciting to lust'. Painters rose to the challenge, representing core doctrines of the faith – transubstantiation, purgatory, the unique status of the Virgin – in cogent painterly form. The period of the Catholic Reformation also saw important changes in artistic manner and technique, the so-called Baroque style of intense emotionalism, employing light and shadow, gesture and movement, to invite the spectator into affective and spiritual identification with the agonies and ecstasies of the lives of Christ and the saints. Bernini's sculpture of 'The Ecstasy of St Teresa' in the Cornaro Chapel of Santa Maria della Vittoria, Rome (into which modern critics invariably read an implied eroticism), exemplifies the Baroque's concern to accentuate the physicality of the human body as a site for the presence of the Holy Spirit. The austerity of reformed Catholicism was well represented in art, for example in the gaunt saints and friars painted by the Spaniards Jusepe Ribera and Francisco de Zurbarán. But increasingly, 17th-century Catholic artists turned to tender and hopeful scenes – the Nativity, the Annunciation, Mary's Immaculate Conception and Assumption – rather than the tortured 'man of sorrows', whose frequent depiction in 15th-century art perhaps reflects the 'salvation anxiety' of late medieval society.

Catholic use of art had its militant, confessional side, an 'up yours' to the iconoclasts. Images of the Virgin decorated military standards, and as 'Our Lady of Victory' she was credited with causing the defeat of the heretics at White Mountain in 1620, and of the Muslims at the crucial naval battle of Lepanto in 1571. Heresy, either a personification, or in the recognizable likeness of Luther or Calvin, was regularly trampled underfoot in triumphant Catholic allegories. Iconoclasm itself could set the terms of new

15. The resplendent 16th-century interior of the church of the Gesú in Rome suggests the Catholic Reformation's confidence in the power of the visual arts to glorify God

devotional relationships with images; there were many tales, particularly in the Spanish Netherlands, of supposedly miraculous statues resisting the attempts of heretics to destroy them. When Francis Drake's sailors desecrated an image of the Virgin Mary during the great raid on Cadiz in 1596, the exiled English priests at Valladolid requested permission as an act of reparation to venerate the statue. The 'Vulnerata' was installed with solemnity in their chapel and became (and remains) the focus of prayers for the conversion of England. In territories undergoing 're-Catholicization', images were tokens of victory and tools of proselytization. Barren churches were re-equipped with statues, altarpieces, and stained-glass windows, paid for as an act of devotion by those eager to prove their Catholic credentials. Further afield, religious art was central to campaigns of conversion in the New World and Asia, areas where the old adage about the didactic role of images in imparting the truths of the faith really applied. The Jesuits in particular had confidence in the ability of art to cross cultural boundaries, though various missionized societies did not merely absorb European Christian models but adapted them to reflect indigenous traditions and circumstances. In Mexico, the image of Our Lady of Guadalupe, in which a distinctly Indian Mary supplanted an original Spanish prototype, became the focus of a thriving cult, and, eventually, a symbol of national identity.

Only an extreme Protestant fringe regarded the second commandment as a blanket ban on all plastic and visual art; English Quakers were unusual in refusing point-blank to have pictures on their walls. The restrictions on religious imagery in Protestant societies did not shut off artistic production, but re-channelled it in other directions. The career of Hans Holbein the Younger (1498–1543) illustrates the theme. When the work for a skilled painter of altarpieces dried up in Basel, Holbein came to England, where his paintings of Tudor courtiers and his iconic full-length portrait of Henry VIII established new standards of realism and characterization. England's native artistic tradition was paltry compared with that of the Netherlands, where the

16. Rembrandt's painting of *Belshazar's Feast* (c. 1636–8) represents a departure in religious painting: biblical scenes as history rather than sacred icons

triumph of Calvinism compelled artists to seek secular patrons and new subjects. Alongside the established field of portraiture, Dutch painters pioneered the art of landscape painting, as well as meticulously observed 'still lifes', and the truthful scenes of everyday life known as genre painting. Artists could not produce paintings for churches, but there was a lively trade in pictures *of* churches, cool and austere architectural studies of ecclesiastical interiors. Religious subject matter was not banished from 17th-century Dutch art, but had to take the form of 'history painting', scenes from the Old Testament which forestalled any temptation to devotional use by focusing on the narration of events with 'genuine' biblical settings and use of costume. Rembrandt van Ryn (1606–69) was the undisputed master of these, giving the lie to any suggestion there is no such thing as Calvinist art.

Nonetheless, there is no question that Protestantism accelerated a separation of art from religion, removing it from an overt role in worship and desacralizing much of its subject matter. The notion of the autonomy of art – a separate sphere of the aesthetic, serving chiefly to inspire admiration and delight – was no concern of the Protestant reformers. But their conviction that artistic representation could in no way express the essence of the divine, or serve as a vehicle for grace, pointed in this direction.

Did art benefit from the development? Perhaps. New vistas opened for the eye, but at the price of accepting that there is no ultimate truth in art. It is by no means evident that Rembrandt was a greater and more original painter than, say, Caravaggio.

Music

'Next to the Word of God, music deserves the highest praise.' Martin Luther was a lover of music, a skilled lutenist, and he saw in song a tool for the breaking down of barriers between clergy and laity and the direct involvement of congregations in worship. Pre-Reformation musical culture was vigorous and varied. There were thriving popular customs of vernacular carol-singing, and, within churches, a rich diet of Latin polyphony (multi-voiced singing in overlapping parts), which for centuries had been edging out the older tradition of monophonic plainsong. Liturgical performance, however, was restricted to clergy and professional or semi-professional choirs. In this context, Luther pioneered a new musical form: the chorale (by permissible anachronism we can call these 'hymns'). Chorales were original verse compositions, set to tunes resembling popular secular songs, and designed to be sung by the entire congregation during services. Luther's *Geistliche Gesangbuchlein* ('little book of spiritual song'), compiled with Johann Walther in 1524, was the first Protestant 'hymn book', a collection of music, in parts, for congregational singing. A later composition of Luther's, *Ein feste Burg ist unser Gott* ('A mighty fortress is our God'), was to be a Protestant favourite for centuries to come. By the end of the 16th century, around 4,000 Lutheran hymns had been published. The Jesuit confessor to Duke Maximilian of Bavaria, Adam Contzen, wrote exasperatedly in 1620 that 'the hymns of Luther have killed more souls than his writings or declamations'. Hymns were eventually to become the common currency of all Christian denominations (*Ein feste Burg* is today even found in Catholic hymnals), but they were a distinctly Lutheran contribution to Christian culture, later exported to other parts of the Protestant world, such as 18th-century England, where aficionados such as Isaac Watts and Charles Wesley perfected the art.

Luther's approach to religious music was permissive. He allowed Latin texts, and admired polyphony. In this respect, he was more cultured than the humanist Erasmus, who had no time for 'thunderous noise and ridiculous confusion of voices', and pedantically thought music should be no more than a vehicle for the clear reception of scriptural text. Subsequent Lutheran music took new and adventurous paths. The addition of solo and instrumental passages to the chorale form contributed to the development of the Oratorio. In the 17th century, the Lutheran composers Heinrich Schütz and Dietrich Buxtehude experimented with a variety of virtuoso forms, including large-scale choral settings of scriptural texts. There is a direct line from Luther's first experiments with chorale to the corpus of their immediate successor, the greatest creative genius of all time, J. S. Bach.

Zwingli can claim no such artistic progeny. Although like Luther a talented musician, he placed music in much the same category as painting: a seductive distraction from unadulterated worship of God. Organs were thrown out of the Zürich churches, and all forms of singing and chant were removed from services. Calvin too rejected organs and instruments, but he and his followers were more responsive to the fact that scripture itself contained injunctions to praise the Lord in song, and provided texts for the purpose: the Psalms of David. The setting of metricized psalms to music became a cultural speciality of the Reformed churches, and their performance a crucial mark of religious identity. There were strict rules: the comprehensibility of the text was paramount, so there was to be no polyphony. Ideally, there should be only one note per syllable (think, if you know it, of the familiar setting of the 'Old Hundredth': All-people-that-on-earth-do-dwell). The result threatened to be dreary, but as habitués of football terraces know, massed unison singing of simple melodies and familiar words can have an inspiring and uplifting effect. The 'Genevan Psalter' compiled under Calvin's and Beza's supervision went through numerous editions and tens of thousands of copies. A key contributor was a French refugee composer, Clement Marot (1497–1544), who had already begun metrical psalm settings in French. Marot's psalms became the battle songs of the Huguenot movement. The fact that psalm texts often express a sense of embattled certitude, and a desire for just retribution against the ungodly, made them a suitable accompaniment to militant resistance on the battlefield. Psalm 68 – 'Let God arise, let his enemies be scattered' – was a favourite of Huguenot armies, as it was later to be of the English parliamentary general Oliver Cromwell. The psalms were also sung congregationally in Reformed worship, often 'lined out' by a precentor, who would suggest the tune and pitch of each line, for the congregation to roar back in response: a practice that can still be heard, in ethereal Gaelic, in the Western Isles of Scotland. In 16th-century England, too, psalm-singing was adopted with alacrity by Protestant congregations, the metrical versions of Thomas Sternhold and John Hopkins being the most frequently published text of the early modern period. That religious conservative and cultural snob Elizabeth I was not, however, a fan, and was reported to have disdained them as 'Geneva jigs'.

Trent's prescriptions for liturgical music resembled its directions about visual art. Church music was to avoid any 'lascivious or impure' associations, and melodies of secular songs were no longer to be used as the basis for liturgical compositions (so-called 'parody masses'). The words should be clear and comprehensible. Yet, paradoxically, the constraints seem to have liberated polyphonic composers of the later 16th century – Lassus, Palestrina, Byrd, Vittoria – to produce some of the most beautiful masses and motets ever written. Sacred music expressed the triumphant and confident face of the Catholic Reformation, and also served as a soundtrack to the aspirations of Catholic secular rulers. St Mark's Basilica in Venice, for example, became an auditorium for the sonic glorification of the republic, where the polychoral (multiple choirs) compositions of Giovanni Gabrieli and Claudio Monteverdi made the most of an extraordinary acoustic. As with the visual image, music played its part in bringing Catholicism to a world stage, and rooting it in home-grown cultures. In both North and South America, hymns were written in native languages, drawing on local melodic traditions. Indigenous singers and instrumentalists were recruited into polyphonic and polychoral performances in Goa and the Philippines, and into the 18th century the New World gave birth to a multitude of locally flavoured baroque compositions, the full scale of which intrepid musicologists are only now uncovering in libraries and diocesan archives across Latin America.

The Reformation was thus itself a polyphonic performance, spawning a variety of musical forms which helped give distinct cultural shape to the emergence and consolidation of rival confessions. There were a few surprising codas. The English Reformation somehow forgot to dismantle the elaborate clerical cohorts staffing the cathedral churches. These continued to stage elaborate sung versions of the various Protestant services, and in due course laid the foundations for a venerable tradition of 'Anglican' choral music. Across the Protestant world, and to a more limited extent the Catholic one, religious music shaped popular culture and was shaped by it. People internalized religious messages as they learned the tunes that carried them, and music was a key expression of social solidarity and communal devotional sentiment. A sad by-product of the decline of church-going in modern Britain is that relatively few people now sing on a regular basis.

Theatre and literature

Any proper assessment of the impact of the Reformation on the development of European literature would require a library of books in itself. There are some 'canonical' works on which the immediate imprint of Reformation theology is deep and obvious: Spenser's *Faerie Queene*, Bunyan's *Pilgrim's Progress*, or Milton's *Paradise Lost*. Yet George Orwell's assertion that 'the novel is practically a Protestant form of art . . . the product of the free mind, of the autonomous individual' is difficult to endorse historically, partly because the Reformation was not noticeably in favour of free minds or autonomous individuals, and partly because some of the best early examples of what we now think of as novels – Miguel Cervantes' *Don Quixote* (1605) or Hans von Grimmelshausen's *Simplicissimus* (1668) – were the work of Catholic authors. Nonetheless, there is no doubt that the ubiquity of Protestant vernacular bible translations supplied a major spur to the spread of literacy, and thus to the eventual development of a reading public. Though the picture is mixed, literacy rates in Catholic states generally lagged behind those in Protestant ones into modern times.

One literary form – the theatre – did not require literacy for participation or appreciation. Later medieval Europe had a sturdy tradition of religious drama: morality plays, with symbolic characters representing vices and virtues; and mystery plays, staging events from the Old Testament and from the life and passion of Christ. Play cycles were deeply entwined with public life and civic identity in the towns of 15th-century France, Germany, and England. It is thus unsurprising that early urban reformers used the genre to spread the Protestant message. The Bernese artist Niklaus Manuel wrote several satirical and anticlerical plays, as did the English evangelical John Bale, adapting the morality format to produce pieces sporting Catholic characters called 'Sedition' and 'Dissimulation'. In Nuremberg, the reformer Hans Sachs (one of Wagner's *Meistersinger*) penned over 200 Protestant plays. In the second half of the 16th century, particularly in England, Protestantism suffered something of a failure of nerve about the theatre, fearing its potential for disorder and depravity. Puritans worried there might be something intrinsically idolatrous about the very act of simulating reality. The disapproval of moralists could not, however, prevent in Elizabethan London a flowering of commercial playhouses, serviced by professional actor-playwrights. As with painting, Protestant unease about the co-mingling of the sacred and the profane freed an art form from the primary function of expressing religious truth and allowed it to mature. This is not, however, to claim that the concerns of the London theatre were 'secular' or unconnected to the cultural formation of a Protestant society. Strongly anti-Catholic themes resonate through works like Marlowe's *The Massacre at Paris*, Webster's *The Duchess of Malfi*, or Middleton's *A Game at Chess*. Religious themes permeate the dramatic works of Shakespeare, though deciding whether Shakespeare's world-view was that of a Protestant, a Catholic, or even an atheist, has become an industry in itself.

The Reformation was, for good or ill, a critical agent of artistic change, a profound determinant of the imaginative possibilities open to the peoples of early modern Europe, and the primary explanation for why the cultural trajectories of modern European countries have developed in such different ways. The extent to which Protestantism represented a paradigmatic shift from the visual to the aural, from the image to the received and spoken Word, can no doubt be exaggerated. But unable to agree on the relationship between methods of representation and the presence of the divine, Catholics and Protestants were left to perceive reality in radically different ways.

Chapter 6
Others

Every year on 5 November, the townspeople of Lewes in East Sussex get together to chant anti-Catholic slogans and burn an effigy of the pope, a business which usually occasions a minor frisson in these politically correct times. It is a continuation of a 17th-century tradition once widespread across England, and an act of symbolic revenge for seventeen Protestant martyrs burned at Lewes in the reign of Mary Tudor. The event (as well as the original episode it commemorates) exemplifies a mentality widespread in the Reformation era, and still with us in various secular and religious guises: a desire to shore up the identity of the majority group by stereotyping and dehumanizing an excluded minority. The unfolding of the Reformation involved contact and confrontation with a series of such alien presences, within and beyond the boundaries of Christian Europe. Examining the fate of these 'others', both real and imagined, enables us to appreciate the extent to which the Reformations were, simultaneously and paradoxically, a channel for intense bigotries and a route to pluralism and social tolerance.

Heretics

On 27 October 1553, Miguel Servetus, a Spanish doctor, was burned to death outside the walls of Geneva. Servetus was an 'anti-trinitarian', who propounded the shocking view that Jesus was not God in human flesh, but simply human, a prophet of the Almighty. If the Calvinists had not caught and burned him, the Catholics would have done it, and there were few respectable people anywhere in Europe who felt he had got less than he deserved. Sebastian Castellio, a Genevan schoolmaster exiled by Calvin, published a text, *Concerning Heretics, whether they are to be persecuted*, arguing that they should not. But this was an eccentric opinion: heresy was the worst of crimes, a crime directly against God. Hanging was literally too good for the heretic, whose body was burned, as a ritual purging of society, and as a symbolic foreshadowing of the flames of hell which would undoubtedly consume the heretic's soul.

From 1523, when two Augustinian friars, members of Luther's order, were burned in Brussels, through to the middle of the 17th century, around 5,000 men and women were judicially executed in Western Europe on account of their religious beliefs. They were executed by state power, working in collaboration with the Church. Most of them, particularly in the early part of the period, were executed by Catholic authorities. Later, Catholics, particularly priests, were put to death by Protestants in England, Ireland, and the Netherlands, though the official rationale tended to be 'treason' rather than 'heresy', in order to maintain the moral high ground of Protestants being the ones who suffered for their faith. Modern ecumenical sensibility extends the title 'martyr' to all of these people, though in the 16th century that would have caused offence all round. Both Catholics and Protestants agreed with the ancient judgement of St Augustine that it is not the fact of the death but the rightness of the cause which makes a martyr (in practice, most of us still concur with this, unwilling, for example, to bestow the title of 'martyr' on Islamic suicide bombers). One group's execution of a heretic was another's heroic death of a martyr, and the same events were read and commemorated in radically different ways. Martyrdoms defined and divided the differing camps; there was no going back from them on either side. The final words of the Reformation's first martyrs, Hendrik Vos and Johann van den

Esschen, spoke for the mentality of all who accepted death rather than recant: 'we believe in God and in one Christian Church. But we do not believe in your church.' By definition, martyrs were those with adamantine convictions, and in eliminating them, rather than persuading them to cave in, the persecuting authorities were admitting a kind of defeat. Martyrs, and would-be martyrs, were a small minority of all religious groups, but a minority with the power to force the pace and confound compromise. They were intensely memorialized, as shining symbols of the cause and an encouragement to the weaker brethren. The printing press played a significant part in this: Catholic Europe wept with pride and anger over detailed engravings depicting the barbarities inflicted on missionary priests by Elizabeth I's government; French Huguenots read about the witness of their martyrs in the

17. A woodcut from Foxe's *Book of Martyrs* of seven Protestants burned together at Smithfield in 1556. Examination of surviving copies suggests that such stirring pictures were the most heavily studied part of Foxe's text

compilation of Jean Crespin, and English Protestants, from the 16th century through to the 19th and beyond, grew up on the stories and vivid pictures in John Foxe's *Book of Martyrs*.

Yet the great majority of people burned to death for religion were not to be found in the pages of magisterial Protestant martyrologies. This was because they were anabaptists who had died for the 'wrong' reasons, and Protestant governments were nearly as resolute as Catholic ones in hunting down and punishing representatives of this loose and disparate phenomenon, for which 'movement' is too precise a description. The Reformation first turned judicially on its own in 1527, when Felix Mantz was executed at Zürich. He was, in a characteristic gesture of Swiss Protestant authorities, not burned but drowned, a brutally droll commentary on adult rebaptism. The intensity of hostility to anabaptists allows us to read back the social and political importance to established authority of the values and practices the anabaptists rejected. Beyond often denying foundational doctrines, like the divinity of Christ, or the Trinity, anabaptists appeared shockingly antisocial, threatening the very fabric of Christian society. Believing that only members of their sect could be saved, they repudiated the conventional teaching that Church and state were the complementary faces of a single Christian community. Instead, they opted out, repudiating duties of military service and refusing the oath-swearing that underpinned the operations of courts, and the obligations of citizenship and guild membership, in all early modern towns. Their assertion of adult baptism symbolized the desire to create a parallel society of their own. Most anabaptists, particularly later in the 16th century, were pacifists, but anabaptism had its militant side, and in 1534–5 was responsible for a shocking episode – a '9/11' moment that fixed the stereotype of danger and deviancy in the minds of all right-thinking Christians. In alliance with refugees from the Netherlands, a group of anabaptists violently seized control of the episcopal town of Münster in northwest Germany. Their leader crowned himself king of a new Jerusalem. Private property was abolished and civic records destroyed. With an over-supply of women in the town, polygamy was declared compulsory. It is a measure of how severely the established powers were rattled that the Protestant Philip of Hesse assisted the Catholic Bishop Franz von Waldeck in retaking the town. In the years after Münster, anabaptism was more or less persecuted out of existence in Germany, Switzerland, and Austria. It survived longer in Eastern Europe, where the followers of Jakob Hutter practised community of goods in their own structured communities. In the 18th and 19th centuries, these and other anabaptists emigrated to America, where Hutterite and Amish descendants still practise a life of austere separation from corrupting worldly society.

Most executions for heresy or Catholic treason preceded 1600. Even as confessional divisions became increasingly clear and rigid, it was apparent in many places that religious minorities could not be persecuted out of existence, though efforts were made to preserve the fiction that only one religion was practised within the boundaries of the state. Non-conformists were tacitly permitted to cross borders on Sundays, a practice that in Germany was called *Auslauf* (running out). Catholics in the Calvinist Palatinate attended mass in the neighbouring bishopric of Speyer, and Lutherans from Habsburg Silesia crossed into Saxony for worship. Alternatively, dissidents might be allowed unofficial places of worship, so long as they gave no outside indication of being a church. Unobtrusive Catholic 'mass houses' proliferated in the backstreets of Irish towns, and Dutch Catholics worshipped in clandestine churches which could be remarkably elaborate on the inside, but from the street looked like ordinary merchants' houses. Some German towns (most prominently, Augsburg) were officially 'bi-confessional'. Here, Lutherans and Catholics competed to advertise their presence in public spaces, using song, processions, and satiric rituals. Possession of a town's principal church was often a source of contention, the solution to which might be to share. To some, this seemed virtually blasphemous, and the papacy fulminated against the dual use of churches in the early

17th century. The practice was nonetheless widespread, though hardly 'ecumenical' in a modern sense. Precise civic regulations controlled when and how each confession could use the building, with the others eagle-eyed for the slightest infringement.

Toleration is not the same as tolerance. The latter is a fundamentally modern attitude, implying acceptance of diversity for its own sake, and an attempt to understand opposing points of view. Dissenters were 'tolerated' not from principle, but for grudging, pragmatic reasons, because peace was usually seen as preferable to religious civil war – the reason for the concession of rights to private worship in the Treaty of Westphalia. Within communities, toleration was a negotiated social practice, and there was no straightforward 'rise of toleration' at the end of the Reformation period. In some respects, traffic was in the opposite direction: intermarriage between Catholics and Protestants in Holland was, for example, less common at the end of the 17th century than at its beginning. Episodes of intense religious violence and intolerance occurred through to the end of the 17th century and into the 18th: Louis XIV's Revocation of the Edict of Nantes, or the 1731 expulsion of a large Lutheran minority from the archbishopric of Salzburg. Yet in the second half of the 18th century, the religious pluralism created by the Reformation did finally receive legal recognition in most of the major monarchies, with the granting of limited civil rights to Catholics in England and Prussia, surviving Huguenots in France, and Lutherans and Calvinists in Habsburg lands.

Muslims and Jews

The religious confrontations and negotiations of Reformation Europe were not necessarily intra-Christian. Neighbouring Islam was the principal political and cultural 'other' of medieval Christian Europe, and while confrontation continued, the Reformation complicated Christianity's relations with the world's other universalizing monotheism. As Protestantism established

itself, European Islam was on the advance in the East and in
retreat in the West. Following the fall of Constantinople in 1453,
Islamic armies pushed into Europe through the Balkans, inflicting
a crushing defeat on the king of Hungary in 1526 and capturing
Buda in 1541. Meanwhile, the Islamic civilization of medieval
Spain had finally crumbled, with the fall of Granada in 1492.
Spanish Muslims were shortly presented with a stark choice:
conversion or expulsion. The majority opted for the former,
without enthusiasm or conviction. Their old Christian neighbours
sneeringly dubbed them 'Moriscos', and the Inquisition closely
scrutinized them for lapses from orthodoxy. From the end of the
15th century, progressive restrictions were placed on traditional
dress and dietary customs, and when Philip II ordered the handing
over of children for education by Christian families, the Morisco
villagers of the Alpujarras exploded in revolt (1568–70). In its
aftermath, the Moriscos were transplanted from Granada, further
away from potential allies in North Africa, and in a large-scale
act of ethnic cleansing were expelled totally from Spain in 1609.
The militancy of Spanish Catholicism owed much to a sense of its
duty to defend the faith on several fronts: against Dutch and
English heretics, against Muslim advances in the Mediterranean,
and against an Islamic fifth column at home. But for other West
Europeans, too, Islam was more than a distant bogeyman. North
African pirates were active throughout the Mediterranean and the
Atlantic seaboard, raiding coastal settlements in Ireland and the
west of England well into the 17th century. It is a remarkable
statistic that around one million West European Christians were
captured and enslaved in Africa between about 1530 and 1640. The
fact that a significant number of these converted to the religion of
their new masters was a recurrent cause of shock and surprise.

Protestants did not generally hail Muslims as brothers-in-arms
against a common Catholic enemy. Indeed, the 1571 victory of
Pius V's Holy League against the Turkish navy at Lepanto was
widely celebrated in Protestant as well as Catholic Europe. Islam
denied the divinity of Christ, and thus, for Luther, Muslims were

simply enemies of God. He did not indulge in any of the crusading rhetoric which continued for centuries, well past its sell-by date, in much of Catholic Europe; force should not be used to advance the gospel. But Luther firmly associated the Ottoman Empire with the coming last days, and the pope and 'the Turk' maintained in his mind a kind of job-share on the position of Antichrist. Some medieval commentators had regarded Islam as a deviant 'Christian sect' with whom common ground could in principle be found. But 'inter-faith dialogue' was not a phrase in Luther's mental lexicon. He helped sponsor a printed Latin translation of the Koran in 1542, not in a spirit of religious openness, but so the views of the enemy could be known and refuted.

Yet Islam played its part in the advance of the Reformation, and not only by diverting Charles V from action against German Protestants, or preventing Philip II's full attention to the Dutch Revolt. In occupied Eastern Europe (and in contrast to reconquered Spain) the Ottomans did not force conversion on their subject peoples, and, happy to see the forces of Christianity divided, did not impede the activities of Protestant missionaries. There was also a degree of curiosity about, and relative sympathy towards, the new faith. The pope, instigator of crusades, was Islam's historic enemy. Calvinism's rejection of religious imagery struck a common chord, as still more did the anti-trinitarians' repudiation of what had always seemed to Muslims the offensive polytheism of Christianity's three-sided God. The most radical anabaptists were in fact safer from persecution in Ottoman territory than in any Christian-controlled state, and the first broadly pluralistic Christian societies were shaped, ironically enough, under the patronage of the Sultan. Curiosity about Islam and Islamic society in the West can be traced through a growing volume of printed texts in the 16th and 17th centuries. Much of this was frankly hostile, or encouraged a voyeuristic and 'Orientalist' interest in slave markets and harems, and in the supposed propensity of Turks for both male and female homosexuality. But, particularly later in the period, other sources made attempts at more impartial and accurate description. Some writers, to highlight the shortcomings of Christian society, even emphasized Turkish 'virtues' of abstinence, charitable giving, and female modesty. Conceivably, ethnographic literature of this sort, once it started to represent Islam in other than apocalyptic terms, helped European Christians to envisage other possible belief systems, and to start recognizing the category of 'religion' as potentially separable from 'society'.

If the Turks were a nearby but external 'other', a mirror to Christian society, Jews represented a different sort of challenge because of their longstanding presence as an irritant foreign body within the *societas Christianorum*. While relations between Christians and Jews had always been difficult, the high and later Middle Ages witnessed an intensification of popular and official hostility, with Jews expelled from England in 1290, France in 1306, Spain (in celebration of the conquest of Granada) in 1492, and Portugal in 1497. Even where Jews were allowed to remain, outbursts of fury against them were a recurrent possibility, often fuelled by the 'blood libel' that Jews kidnapped and murdered Christian boys to use their blood in the baking of Passover bread. A related charge was that of host desecration: Jews were believed to wish to steal consecrated eucharistic wafers in order to torture them, and thus perpetuate their violence against the body of Jesus. Hostility to Jews was often stirred up by the preaching of the friars, but by and large secular and religious authorities sought to restrain popular violence against them, mindful of their importance to the urban economy and state financing arrangements.

Luther's pamphlet of 1523, *That Jesus Christ was Born a Jew*, seemed to promise a new start in relations, urging courteous and kind treatment. This, however, was not respect for difference but a conversion strategy, and similar approaches had been advocated before. Not only did Jews not turn to the gospel, but news reaching Luther of a radical sect in Moravia advocating the readoption of

Saturday as the Christian day of observance seemed to presage a Jewish revival. Luther's *On the Jews and their Lies* (1543) makes for depressing reading: he advocated the confiscation and destruction of the Talmud (compilations of Jewish laws and traditions), the prohibition of rabbinic teaching, the burning of synagogues, and expulsions. The vitriol behind this text was theological, not 'racial' in our modern sense, but it was to be favoured reading in 1930s Germany. Some reformers felt Luther had gone too far, yet none moved beyond the position that Jews were at best wilfully perverse in spurning the offer of the gospel. Indeed, it was a staple of Protestant propaganda that papists and Jews were remarkably similar, in thrall to 'works-righteousness', and obsessed with rituals and rules.

If the Reformation provided no new dawn for Jews, the Sun was setting further in the Catholic world. Paul IV, the most unbending of Counter-Reformation popes, forced the Jews of Rome into a ghetto in 1555, amidst seizure and burning of Talmudic writings. Italian Jews were ghettoized almost everywhere in the course of the following century – an expression of Tridentine zeal, but also an opportunity for secular rulers to supervise Jewish economic activity more effectively. Catholic intolerance was most acute in Spain, which in theory had solved its 'Jewish problem' at a stroke in 1492, but in fact employed a governmental industry – the Spanish Inquisition and its army of informers – to check for backsliding on the part of 'New Christians', or *conversos*. The Inquisition burned about 2,000 'judaisers' in its first half-century between 1480 and 1530, the only period for which it really deserves its bloodthirsty reputation. The processes were arbitrary, but bureaucratic and evidence-based, so *conversos* were at least prosecuted for the real 'crimes' of avoiding pork or observing the Jewish Sabbath, rather than for such fantasy transgressions as ritual murder or defilement of the host. Anti-Jewish sentiments in 16th-century Spain were enshrined in legislation requiring non-Jewish ancestry, *limpieza de sangre* (purity of blood), as a condition for the holding of ecclesiastical office. Philip II endorsed the development with the comment that 'all the heresies in Germany, France, and Spain have been sown by descendants of Jews', but it was opposed by the Jesuits, and in the early 17th century by the Inquisition itself. Some historians have identified Spain as the birthplace of modern racial 'anti-Semitism', but since the antagonisms were overtly religious in nature it seems safer to speak of anti-Judaism.

Well into the 16th century there were few signs that the position of Jews in Europe was changing for anything but the worse. But ultimately the Reformation opened spaces for Judaism to breathe more easily. Inquisitorial scepticism about host desecration was shared in Protestant societies for the simple reason that the denial of transubstantiation rendered the fantasy culturally meaningless. Some places of settlement closed to Jews began to reopen. The Habsburg emperors Maximilian II and Rudolph II allowed Jews to settle in Bohemia at the end of the 16th century, and a few decades later, Cromwell's Protectorate readmitted them to England. Yet it was the diverse society of the Dutch Republic, where the authorities asked few questions about the private practice of faith, which offered the most attractive destination. New Christians from Portugal and Spain began emigrating there in large numbers in the early 17th century, and quietly returned to the faith of their ancestors. These 'Sephardic' Jews shared the strongly anti-Catholic sentiments of Calvinist society, and also regarded Reformed Protestantism as a welcome, though deficient, return to the values of the Hebrew bible. For their part, Protestants' extensive scriptural reading, as both edification and entertainment, laid the basis for a more positive assessment of Jewish neighbours, who might now remind them more of the heroic figures of the Old Testament than of the vengeful Pharisees of the New. The Protestant vogue for scriptural names – Abraham, Benjamin, Daniel – probably also helped to muddy a sense of the total otherness of the Jew. The attempted realism of Protestant history painting tended in a similar direction. In a radical break with traditional iconography, Rembrandt's 1645 painting of the Holy

Family portrayed Mary as a recognizably Jewish mother, reading a Hebrew book while rocking her son's cradle.

Pagans

The most perplexing confrontations with the non-Christian other took place not within, or even on the borders of, Christian Europe, but far overseas, as the imperatives of Reformation caused Catholics (and belatedly, Protestants) to carry the message of Christ to distant lands. Those who did so never doubted the truth of the ancient adage, *extra ecclesiam nulla salus* ('there is no salvation outside the Church'). This, the ultimate exclusionary statement, was also an urgent call to inclusion, to work tirelessly to convert pagans and save their souls from eternal damnation. The opportunities were almost literally boundless. But how was conversion to be accomplished, and what if any concessions were to be made to the expectations of host cultures in the process? These dilemmas forced Catholic missionaries to confront questions about what was fundamental to Christianity which were in their way no less profound than those pondered by Luther and Calvin. Remarkably, it did not generally prompt them to ask why, if Christianity was the only door to salvation, God had created millions of souls that for centuries had no opportunity to experience it.

The first major missionary venture was a story in miniature of the successes and screw-ups attending Catholic evangelism beyond Europe. The Portuguese establishment of trading posts along the coast of West Africa at the end of the 15th century netted a few local converts, and one very big fish, the ruler of the powerful kingdom of Kongo, Nzinga Nkuvu, who in 1491 (a year before Columbus) accepted baptism as João I. He had evidently not read all the small print, however, and rejected Christianity after tiring of the missionaries' insistence on the burning of fetish objects and the restriction to just one wife (a prescription with profound social and political implications). Yet one of his sons, Mvemba Nzinga

(Afonso I), remained fervently Christian, and reigned for 39 years. For a century, Kongo was a thriving Catholic African kingdom, but the attempts of the Portuguese crown to control appointments of bishops produced a crippling shortage of clergy, and with the political collapse of the kingdom in the 17th century Kongolese Catholicism effectively fused with native religion. Hampering the Portuguese efforts to spread Christianity more widely and deeply in West Africa was European sponsorship of the burgeoning slave trade. It would be long after the close of the Reformation period before any kind of consensus emerged that Christian faith was incompatible with slavery.

Questions of the intrinsic value of human beings were, however, debated earnestly during the evangelization of the Americas. Cortes' and Pizarro's destruction of the Aztec and Inca empires was a political *fait accompli*, but some churchmen saw the subsequent exploitation of native labour by conquistador landlords as a barrier to missionary work. Others, including the leading Spanish humanist Juan de Sepulveda, inclined to the view that Indians fitted Aristotle's category of the 'natural slave': they were incapable of free will, and thus the legitimate targets of 'just war'. In 1550, he debated the issue at Valladolid in the presence of Charles V against a fellow Dominican, Bartolomé de las Casas, an indefatigable critic of the crimes of the conquistadors and passionate advocate of the rights of indigenous peoples. The result was inconclusive, but the Spanish crown was inclined to protect 'its' Indian subjects from exploitation by self-aggrandizing settlers, and the papacy had already affirmed in a bull of 1537 that Indians were entitled to liberty and to own property. The early years of evangelization in the Americas, largely undertaken by the friars, were full of optimism, as thousands willingly received baptism. But disillusionment at the level of converts' religious understanding began to set in, and in 1555 a Mexican provincial council forbade the ordaining of Indians to the priesthood, a barrier not broken in Latin America until 1794. Suspicions that his Mayan charges were still secretly worshipping idols led the Franciscan Provincial in

Yucatan, Diego de Landa, to launch a vicious inquisitorial campaign over three months in 1562, in the course of which thousands of Indians were tortured (over 150 dying in the process) before Landa was removed from office.

It would be crass to maintain, however, that Amerindians (or the inhabitants of the Philippines in the same period) typically 'rejected' Christianity, or continued self-consciously to preserve traditional beliefs under a cynical veneer of official Catholicism. Rather, they adopted the new faith on terms that made sense to them, accentuating some aspects and downplaying others. Churches occupied the sites of temples, and served comparable functions as centres of ceremonial and community life. Public festivals, outdoor processions, and the patronage of guardian saints all resonated with established ways of doing things, and the Mexican 'Day of the Dead', involving the placing of food and drink as offerings on family graves, exemplifies a syncretic fusion between pre-conquest practices and Catholic celebration of the Feast of All Souls.

Christianity faced different challenges among the ancient civilizations of the Far East, where there were few military conquests to argue the powerlessness of the old gods. In India, the Portuguese made some progress in the vicinity of their coastal bases, including mass conversion of the Paravas, fishing people of the Coromandel Coast, who sought European help against Muslim raiders. But beyond the Portuguese enclaves, Christianity was generally disdained as a low-caste and foreign phenomenon. Attempts to widen its appeal in the East, especially to social elites, were pioneered by Francis Xavier (1506–52), an original Jesuit companion of Loyola's. As a missionary in Japan, Xavier took the 'adaptionist' line that local traditions not directly contrary to Christianity were to be embraced, and laid the foundations for a thriving Japanese Church. Another Jesuit, Roberto Nobili, developed the approach in India, dressing and eating as a high-caste Brahmin, and sanctioning such 'social' customs for

Le Père Matthieu Ricci.

18. The Italian Jesuit Matteo Ricci (1551–1610) encouraged Christian accommodation with local culture, and here strikes the pose of a Chinese Mandarin

Christian converts as ritual bathing and the wearing on the body of sacred ashes. The accommodationist technique was also employed by Jesuits in China, where Matteo Ricci (1551–1610) and his successors dressed like Mandarins, impressing the scholarly Chinese administrative class with their cartographic and astronomical skills. In an effort to suggest that Christianity was not an alien import, but the perfection of existing principles, Ricci encouraged the use of roughly analogous Chinese terms for concepts such as 'God' and 'heaven', and argued that Confucian ancestor worship was a civil ceremony fully compatible with Catholicism.

All of these efforts bore fruit: there was unspectacular but steady growth of Christian communities in India, Ceylon, Vietnam, and China, and more dramatic expansion in Japan, under the patronage of regional barons, or *daimyos*, before it was terminated by the onset of an intense and cruel political persecution. The congregation of *Propaganda Fidei* showed in the 17th century remarkable openness to the notion that native customs must be respected. But Jesuit methods were opposed by rival missionary groups, especially the Dominicans, who lobbied avidly against them in Europe. In 1704, after years of prevarication, the papacy prohibited 'Chinese rites', causing massive offence at the Manchu imperial court, and stifling the expansion of Christianity in China. The global expansion of Catholic Christianity was nonetheless a success story, but one that raised fundamental questions about the nature of the exercise. The struggles of Protestant reformers in Europe to decide what was 'adiaphora' paled alongside the calculations made by Jesuits in India and China. Subsequent history proved the missionaries right to believe that Christianity need not be so identified with the norms of European society that it was incapable of speaking meaningfully to peoples in other parts of the world (and in fact there were already centuries-old non-European Christian communities – in the Middle East, in Ethiopia, in China, and among the Syrian-Malabar, or 'St Thomas Christians', of India). But if the 'essence' of Christianity was detachable from social and cultural structures in Asia, might that not ultimately be true of Europe itself? The valorizing, for purposes of evangelization, of the customs and rituals of strange societies may have had unforeseen and long-term consequences, fostering among European intellectuals a cultural and religious relativism to which Christianity itself was eventually subject.

Witches

One outsider to Christian society could not be accommodated, tolerated, or negotiated with: the witch. The belief that certain persons possess magical powers which they employ for evil and destructive purposes is known to many cultures, and was commonplace in the Middle Ages. But, contrary to careless popular usage, the large-scale pursuit and punishment of witches in Europe was not a 'medieval' phenomenon, but an aspect of early modernity. Over a period starting in the late 15th century, gathering pace after c. 1560 and drawing to a close in the early 18th century, around 100,000 people (mostly women) were judicially accused of witchcraft in Europe. Of these, perhaps 40,000 were put to death, a figure significantly larger than the number of those executed for religious unorthodoxy in the same epoch, but much smaller than the death-rate for other, more tangible crimes, such as murder or serious theft. The relationship between the Reformation and what is sometimes sensationally termed the 'European witch craze' is a complex one. The chronology loosely fits, though intense witch-hunting preceded the onset of the Reformation, and actually died down during its first generation. In spite of often extreme religious rhetoric, Catholics and Protestants generally did not accuse each other of witchcraft. Nor was the principal charge against witches directly linked to major Reformation controversies. Villagers had always suspected antisocial old women of spell-casting and malevolent cursing, but what created a dynamic of official persecution was the growing conviction of theologians that witches constituted a vast army of apostates, who had sworn allegiance to the devil and under his command were at war with Christian society.

It seems unlikely, however, that witch-hunting would have developed in the way or with the ferocity it did without the background of religious conflict. The period of most intense persecution, the two to three decades either side of 1600, coincided

19. A diabolic baptism, from Francesco Maria Guazzo's *Compendium maleficarum* (1626): theologians were inclined to imagine witchcraft as an organized and ritualistic 'counter-church'

with the confessionalization of Protestant and Catholic states, and the most intense bouts of ideological warfare. There was a heightened sense of the need for societal purity and uniformity, which manifested itself in action against these most abnormal of deviants, as well as an apocalyptic atmosphere which directed attention to the machinations of the devil. Whether Catholics or Protestants did more to ramp up the persecution is a moot point. The worst offenders were Catholic prince-bishops of generally small German territories: in 1616–17 over 300 witches were burned by the bishop of Würzburg, Julius Echter von Mespelbrünn, a stalwart of Catholic Reform. But some of the lowest rates of execution were in Catholic southern Europe, where the Spanish Inquisition, like its Roman cousin, was sceptical about the deeds ascribed to witches. Few witches were burned in Calvin's Geneva, and there were virtually no trials in the Protestant

Netherlands or the Calvinist Palatinate. But other Calvinist territories, notably Scotland, witnessed some of the most intense persecutions anywhere, continuing into the 1660s. While witch trials were generally on the wane from the middle of the 17th century, there were nasty outbreaks in English East Anglia during the closing stages of the Civil War, in Lutheran Sweden in 1668–76, and, famously, in the exported Puritan community of Salem, Massachusetts, as late as 1692. A compound alchemy of factors brought the witch trials to a close: more exacting standards of proof in various legal systems, and restrictions on the use of torture, scientific scepticism, and an increased elitist reluctance to take seriously the frenzied accusations of grubby villagers. But the end of religious warfare and halting steps towards pluralism were important parts of the story. As real 'others' were grudgingly accepted and integrated into European societies, the imaginary ones lost their existential menace – another indication of the Reformation's failure to create rigidly uniform Christian communities, and its accidental success in generating something else.

Chapter 7
Legacy

This book began by suggesting that Reformation created the Europe we recognize today. A sceptic posing the rhetorical question 'what has the Reformation ever done for us?' is still likely to hear in reply a litany of monumental achievements: modern capitalism, the concept of political freedom, the advancement of science, the decline of magic and superstition. All of these have long been regarded as the precocious and unruly children of the (Protestant) Reformation. However, things are not so clear-cut, and the Reformation's imagined role as mother of modernity raises thorny issues about parentage and nurture. As a religious movement, the Reformation was fundamentally concerned with old not new questions, and Luther himself, one suspects, would vigorously contest any paternity suit the modern age might bring against him.

The relationship between our world and Luther's revolution seemed more straightforward in the days when scholars generally subscribed to a notion of 'progress' in human affairs, a benevolent and linear historical journey in which the Reformation served as mile-stone not millstone. Although his ideas are sometimes simplistically misrepresented, the late 19th-century German sociologist Max Weber proposed the influential theory that 'the Protestant ethic', specifically its Calvinist and Puritan forms, encouraged the 'spirit of capitalism': material success was interpreted by anxious Calvinists as a possible sign of election to salvation. The evident economic advances enjoyed by England and the Dutch Republic in the 17th and 18th centuries offer some support for the thesis, but recent historians have largely come away unpersuaded. There was no necessary connection between Calvinistic culture and capitalistic prosperity, as the backward condition of godly Scotland testifies. The 17th-century dominance of the Atlantic powers (including Catholic France) more plausibly looks like part of a longer-term economic and political shift away from the Mediterranean, in the wake of Ottoman expansion from the 15th century onwards.

Another of Weber's modernizing concepts now seems less persuasive than once it did: the notion that Protestantism, as a transcendent and rationalistic religion, fatally undermined supernatural and magical beliefs about the lived environment, and promoted a far-reaching 'disenchantment of the world'. It is true that – officially – the Protestant Reformation set its face against the inherent sacral power of objects and rituals, the intermediate spiritual agency of the saints, and the notion of 'sacred' times and spaces disrupting the predictable rhythms and patterns of God's created universe. But right across Protestant Europe, and into modern times, scholars have found evidence of religious cultures saturated with the presence of the supernatural, alive with signs and portents, and the imagined activity of demons and angels. Protestant villagers, like Catholic ones, continued to rely on quasi-magical rituals to protect themselves from evil forces or to cure disease, they believed in ghosts and poltergeists, and they saw sacred significance in particular days and seasons. This was not just the failure of 'ignorant' people to grasp the true meaning of the Protestant message. The usual Protestant teaching on miracles was that they became unnecessary with the establishment of the early Church and writing of the bible: the 'age of miracles' ended after the time of the apostles, and the Catholic 'miracles' of recent times were frauds or delusions. But Protestant intellectuals shared with the common people an intense interest in 'providence' – the signs of God's will, favour, or displeasure that could be inferred from strange occurrences in the natural world, such as the oak tree in late Elizabethan Essex which for three days moaned like a dying man, and was interpreted locally as a warning from God against sinfulness and pride. In practice, remarkable providential events were not so very different from the traditional miracle, a word which steadily seeped back into Protestant vocabulary over the course of the Reformation period.

The acceptability of the notion of miracles, along with belief in the intervention of the devil and other spiritual powers in human affairs, did come increasingly under strain, in educated circles at least, as a concomitant of the phenomenon conventionally shrink-wrapped with the label 'the Scientific Revolution'. This epoch of remarkable if sporadic intellectual advances – encompassing the discovery of the circulation of blood around the human body, and of the Earth around the Sun – coincides almost exactly with the period of the Reformations, but the nature of their dependence on each other is difficult to pin down. Protestantism's sponsorship of modern science is in some circles as axiomatic as Catholicism's hostility to it. The 1633 papal condemnation of Galileo for the 'heresy' of teaching that the Earth revolves around the Sun is for many people an iconic moment in the history of intellectual freedom. Yet Galileo was no Protestant, but a devout Catholic, as was Nicolas Copernicus (1473–1543), the original proponent of the heliocentric theory, and René Descartes (1596–1650), the French philospher whose thesis that the created universe was a kind of machine severely problematized the role within it of spirits and occult forces. Some Catholic thinkers continued discreetly to teach heliocentrism even after the Galileo condemnation (an affair in which politics and personalities played as great a role as any clash of fundamental principles). Catholic universities were centres of some of the most advanced 'scientific' learning, and the expertise of the Jesuits in astronomy was highly prized as far away as the Ming and Manchu courts of China.

It is undoubtedly true that there was more scope for scientists (or as they were called at the time, natural philosophers) to develop innovative theories in some parts of the Protestant world – for example, 17th-century England – than in parts of the Catholic one, such as Inquisitorial Spain. But the notion of Protestantism as a precondition for science is a specious one, not least because of the lively traditions of speculation and experiment to be found in medieval Europe. The beating heart of Protestantism was not in any case unfettered enquiry, but deference to an authoritative text, and throughout our period there were plenty of Protestants who opposed heliocentrism on the basis of the Book of Joshua's reference to the Sun 'standing still' at Gibeon, just as today plenty of Protestants oppose evolution on the basis of the Creation account in Genesis. Christian fundamentalism has its roots in the certainties of the Reformation.

Protestant intellectuals in the 17th and 18th centuries were by no means all inflexible scriptural literalists. There was a real effort in some quarters to find explanations for biblical miracles consistent with the laws of nature, and to promote a 'natural theology' in which God's creation and governance of the universe could be seen to be entirely rational and reasonable. It has become almost obligatory to point out that luminaries of scientific discovery, such as Isaac Newton and Robert Boyle, respective fathers of modern physics and chemistry, were deeply religious men who saw no contradiction between their faith and their work. Yet the reluctance of nearly all natural philosophers of the Reformation era to differentiate 'science' and 'religion' as modes of explanation may ultimately have done religion no favours. In the long term, it encouraged a perception of the incompatibility of religion and science, when some of the presumptions about the creation of the world on which early modern science had based itself were shown in due course to be simply untenable. Modern Darwinism seems less a culmination of Reformation scientific insights than a thorough-going refutation of them.

What then, amidst all these discordant notes, is left of the Reformation's claim to be the resounding overture to the modern world? The final suggestion of this book is that if the melody is still to ring out loudly, its key-signature should be sought not so much in the inherent qualities of Protestantism (or Tridentine Catholicism) as in the dynamic interplay of forces conjured up by the Reformation era, and in the laws of unintended consequences. The most significant outcomes of the Reformation can in fact be expressed as a succession of paradoxes. The Reformations, Protestant and Catholic, aimed at the creation of social and religious uniformity, and ended up producing forms of pluralism that were subsequently exported to, and replicated in, the farthest-flung parts of the world. They promised to intensify the political and spiritual power of the state, and yet they generated a grammar and vocabulary by which its authority could be challenged. They sought to eradicate heresy and false belief, but falteringly permitted the toleration of error to a previously undreamt-of degree. They set out to sacralize the whole of society, and ended up creating the long-term conditions for its secularization.

These are all ways of saying that the principal legacies of the Reformation were the fact of division, and the emergence of strategies for coping with that fact. The medieval ideal of a unified 'Christendom' – a family of local societies fully integrated within and between each other by shared Christian political and social values – was perhaps always more of an aspiration than a reality. But the Reformations, by advancing irreconcilable schemes for how humans should try to reconcile themselves to God, permanently shattered both the aspiration and its dim reflection in social practice. The period of intense confessionalization and prolonged religious warfare nurtured the hope that a new unitary ideal could be imposed on society by persuasion and force of arms, and in a few places that ambition was temporarily achieved. But total victory eluded all sides in Europe's home-grown clash of civilizations. When the convulsions stopped, in about 1700, the patterns of the kaleidoscope were intricate and dappled. Protestants were a large minority in Western Europe as a whole, and dominant in much of its northern half. But (other than in the confessionally homogeneous kingdoms of Lutheran Scandinavia) Protestant societies often contained substantial Catholic, Jewish, or radical minorities, as well as reflecting the permanent split between the confessional traditions of Lutheran and Reformed. The Mediterranean societies of Catholic Southern Europe were less diverse, but officially Catholic territories in Central and Eastern Europe, as well as in France, contained many open or covert dissidents. Moreover, all the Reformations had spawned their own more rigorous internal reformations, with the emergence of Lutheran 'pietists' and Catholic Jansenists, and the seeping out of the non-conformities of Presbyterians, Baptists, and Quakers from the wounds of the doctrinally unstable Church of England. With considerable significance for the future, Europe's plural patterning was evident already in the fledgling colonies of what would later become the United States of America: Puritan Massachusetts, Episcopalian Virginia, Catholic Maryland, Quaker Pennsylvania.

The religious stalemate in Europe and America had consequences for what we can recognize as the emergence of the 'secular' state and the practice of religion within it. If no single religious ideal was able to serve as the unifying and integrative principle of society, then shared identities, rights, and obligations had to be reconstituted on some other basis, like respect for an abstract concept of law, or common national pride. Social peace required practical toleration of religious difference, and a renegotiation of religion's relationship to public and community life. Modern Europe's pluralistic and broadly tolerant society does not represent an inevitable triumph of progress, but the specific historical outcome of a contested religious past. If religion gradually ceased to be the official ideology of the state, and faith a necessary badge of citizenship, then increasingly it lent itself to domestication and privatization. It also, inevitably, began to acquire an optional character. When the state no longer by law required people to attend a particular church, then some seized the opportunity not to frequent places of worship at all. When the state ceased to support the religious authorities in sanctioning prosecutions for heresy, a few intellectuals abandoned orthodox Christianity altogether. Some adopted the religious philosophy known as 'Deism', which rejected 'revealed' truths such as the Trinity and divinity of Jesus, denied all manifestations of the supernatural, and held that God was knowable only through the application of reason to his immutable laws of nature. A handful of atheists went further, openly questioning whether religious belief of any sort was either necessary or true. We should be wary of exaggerated claims about 'secularization' in Europe, in the sense of widespread indifference about religious truth, or any dramatic social marginalization of the Christian churches. Such phenomena are hardly discernible before at least the end of the 18th century. Atheists were a tiny minority even in Enlightenment Europe, and Christian belief and practice remained normative for most Europeans well into the 20th century. At the close of the early modern period, religion remained an important part of many people's identity, but increasingly perhaps it did so as a component of a more variegated whole, just as religion itself was starting to become a discrete component of society and not its basic structure and grammar. Even within ostensibly united confessional cultures, religion was losing traction in the decades around 1700 as a vehicle for shared meanings across society as a whole. Economic and educational changes were widening social divides, and some members of the elite felt an increasing need to distance themselves from the beliefs of the common people, to scoff at religious 'enthusiasm', and to express scepticism about witches, miracles, and demonstrations of divine providence. The tendency was more marked in Protestant societies, but was not absent from Catholic ones.

The Reformations, Protestant and Catholic, thus made the modern world in spite of themselves, and their founding fathers would neither have expected nor welcomed the eventual outcomes. Even

Chronology

1519	Luther debates Johan Eck in Leipzig; Charles V becomes Holy Roman Emperor
1520	Luther excommunicated and burns papal bull
1521	Luther defies Emperor at Diet of Worms and is hidden by Frederick the Wise at Wartburg
1522	Luther's translation of New Testament; Zwingli presides over Lent sausage meal in Zürich; Luther reverses Karlstadt's innovations in Wittenberg
1523	Two Augustinian friars burned in Brussels: first Reformation martyrs
1524	Luther and Johan Walter produce first Protestant 'hymn book'
1523-6	Reformation in Zürich
1524-5	Peasants' War in Germany
1525	Luther marries Katharina von Bora; Erasmus breaks with Luther over freedom of the will
1526	Turkish victory at Mohács in Hungary; William Tyndale's English New Testament printed
1527	First Anabaptist executed by reformers (at Zürich); Gustav Vasa of Sweden declares independence from Rome
1529	'Protestatio' at Diet of Speyer gives its name to 'Protestants'; failure of Luther and Zwingli to agree over Eucharist at Colloquy of Marburg; first religious war in Switzerland
1530	Augsburg Confession supplies Lutheran statement of faith
1531	Lutheran League of Schmalkalden against Charles V; death of Zwingli in second Swiss religious war
1532-5	Henry VIII breaks with Rome and becomes 'Supreme Head' of Church of England
1534	Francis I imposes crackdown on Protestants in France; flight of Calvin; Ignatius Loyola founds Society of Jesus; Kildare Rebellion in Ireland
1534-5	Anabaptist kingdom of Münster
1536	Publication of Calvin's *Institutes*; beginnings of Calvinist reformation in Geneva; Lutheran Reformation established in Denmark; Pilgrimage of Grace against Henry VIII
1540	Society of Jesus recognized by pope

1542	Establishment of Roman Inquisition
1543	Luther's pamphlet *On the Jews and their Lies*
1545-7	First session of Council of Trent
1546-7	Schmalkaldic War
1547	Death of Luther; defeat of Lutheran princes at Mühlberg; death of Henry VIII and Protestant regime established in England under Edward VI
1548	Augsburg Interim re-imposes Catholicism in Empire
1550	Rights of Amerindians debated at Valladolid
1551-2	Second session of Council of Trent
1553	Burning of Servetus in Geneva; Mary I restores Catholicism in England
1555	Peace of Augsburg: *cuius regio eius religio*
1556	Abdication of Charles V
1558	Death of Mary I and accession of (Protestant) Elizabeth I in England
1559	Death of Henry II of France; Calvinist National Synod in Paris; papal Index of forbidden books
1559-60	Religious revolution in Scotland inspired by John Knox
1562	Outbreak of religious civil war in France (continues intermittently to 1598); *de facto* religious toleration in Poland; persecution of Christian 'back-sliders' in Yucatan, Mexico
1562-3	Third session of Council of Trent
1563	Frederick III establishes Calvinism in German Palatinate; first edition of John Foxe's *Book of Martyrs*
1564	Death of Calvin; birth of Shakespeare; birth of Galileo
1566	Iconoclasm in the Netherlands
1567	Start of Dutch Revolt against Spain
1568	Mary Queen of Scots flees to England; revolt of the Moriscos (converted Muslims) in Spain
1570	Pope Pius V excommunicates Elizabeth I
1571	Naval victory of Christian forces against Turks at Lepanto
1572	St Bartholomew's Day Massacre in Paris

1577	Formula of Concord reunites German Lutherans
1579	Philippe du Plessis-Mornay's *Vindication Against Tyrants* justifies overthrow of ungodly rulers
1582	Gregory XIII reforms the calendar
1584	Huguenot Henry of Navarre becomes heir to the French throne
1589	Assassination of Henry III of France: Henry of Navarre succeeds as Henry IV
1593	Henry IV converts to Catholicism
1598	Edict of Nantes declares limited toleration for Huguenots in France
1603	Death of Elizabeth I and accession of James I, uniting Scottish and English crowns
1605	Gunpowder Plot to blow up English Parliament
1609	Expulsion from Spain of the Moriscos
1616-17	Intense witch persecution in bishopric of Würzburg
1618	Outbreak of Thirty Years War
1619	Synod of Dort (Netherlands) condemns deviations from Calvinism
1622	Establishment of papal congregation *Propaganda Fide* (for missions)
1629	Ferdinand II's Edict of Restitution bans Calvinism in Empire and provokes entry of Sweden to Thirty Years War
1633	Galileo condemned for heresy by Inquisition; Vincent de Paul and Louise de Marillac found Daughters of Charity
1638	National Covenant in defence of Reformation signed in Scotland
1641	Catholic rebellion in Ireland
1642	Outbreak of Civil War in England
1648	Treaty of Westphalia ends Thirty Years War and enacts religious toleration in the Empire
1649	Execution of Charles I of England
1660	Restoration of Charles II and re-establishment of the Anglican Church

1685	Louis XIV revokes Edict of Nantes
1688-9	'Glorious Revolution' deposes Catholic James II in Britain and Ireland; toleration for (Protestant) non-Anglicans
1692	Witch persecution in Salem, Massachusetts
1702-11	Huguenot rebellion in France
1704	Papal prohibition of 'Chinese Rites'
1731	Expulsion of Lutherans from archbishopric of Salzburg

Further reading

General

R. Bireley, *The Refashioning of Catholicism 1450–1700* (Basingstoke, 1999).

J. Bossy, *Christianity in the West 1400–1700* (Oxford, 1985).

E. Cameron, *The European Reformation* (Oxford, 1991).

O. Chadwick, *The Early Reformation on the Continent* (Oxford, 2001).

P. Collinson, *The Reformation* (London, 2003).

F. Fernández-Armesto and D. Wilson, *Reformation: Christianity and the World 1500–2000* (London, 1996).

C. Lindberg, *The European Reformations* (Oxford, 1996).

D. MacCulloch, *Reformation: Europe's House Divided 1490–1700* (London, 2003).

A. Pettegree (ed.), *The Reformation World* (London, 2000).

R. Po-Chia Hsia, *The World of Catholic Renewal 1540–1770* (Cambridge, 1998).

R. Po-Chia Hsia (ed.), *Cambridge History of Christianity*, Volume 6: *Reform and Expansion 1500–1660* (Cambridge, 2007).

U. Rublack, *Reformation Europe* (Cambridge, 2005).

A. Ryrie (ed.), *Palgrave Advances in the European Reformations* (Basingstoke, 2006).

J. D. Tracy, *Europe's Reformations 1450–1650* (Oxford 1999).

P. G. Wallace, *The Long European Reformation* (Basingstoke, 2004).

Salvation

A. E. McGrath, *Reformation Thought: An Introduction* (Oxford, 1988).

D. K. McKim (ed.), *The Cambridge Companion to John Calvin* (Cambridge, 2004).

M. A. Mullett, *Martin Luther* (London, 2004).

H. O. Oberman, *Luther: Man between God and the Devil* (London, 1993).

S. E. Ozment, *The Reformation in the Cities: The Appeal of Protestantism to Sixteenth-Century Germany and Switzerland* (New Haven, CT, 1975).

L. Palmer Wandel, *The Eucharist in the Reformation: Incarnation and Liturgy* (Cambridge, 2006).

B. M. Reardon, *Religious Thought in the Reformation* (London, 1995).

Politics

W. D. J. Cargill Thompson, *The Political Thought of Martin Luther*, ed. P. Broadhead (Brighton, 1984).

J. M. Headley et al. (eds.), *Confessionalization in Europe 1555–1700* (Aldershot, 2004).

M. P. Holt, *The French Wars of Religion, 1562–1629* (Cambridge, 1995).

Q. Skinner, *The Foundations of Modern Political Thought*, Volume 2: *The Age of Reformation* (Cambridge, 1978).

Society

K. von Greyerz, *Religion and Culture in Early Modern Europe 1500–1800* (Oxford, 2008).

P. Matheson (ed.), *Reformation Christianity* (Minneapolis, MN, 2007).

T. M. Safley (ed.), *The Reformation of Charity: The Secular and the Religious in Early Modern Poor Relief* (Leiden, 2003).

B. Scribner and T. Johnson (eds.), *Popular Religion in Germany and Central Europe 1400–1800* (Basingstoke, 1996).

M. Todd, *The Culture of Protestantism in Early Modern Scotland* (New Haven, CT, 2002).

M. E. Wiesner-Hanks, *Christianity and Sexuality in the Early Modern World* (London, 2000).

Culture

C. M. N. Eire, *War Against the Idols: The Reformation of Worship from Erasmus to Calvin* (Cambridge, 1986).

S. Michalski, *The Reformation and the Visual Arts: The Protestant Image Question in Western and Eastern Europe* (Abingdon, 1993).

M. O'Connell, *The Idolatrous Eye: Iconoclasm and Theater in Early-Modern England* (Oxford, 2000).

A. Pettegree, *Reformation and the Culture of Persuasion* (Cambridge, 2005).

Others

M. Bodian, *Hebrews of the Portuguese Nation: Conversos and Community in Early Modern Amsterdam* (Bloomington, 1997).

F. Cervantes, *The Devil in the New World: The Impact of Diabolism in New Spain* (New Haven, CT, 1994).

B. S. Gregory, *Salvation at Stake: Christian Martyrdom in Early Modern Europe* (Cambridge, MA, 1999).

H. Kamen, *The Spanish Inquisition: A Historical Revision* (New Haven, CT, 1998).

B. J. Kaplan, *Divided by Faith: Religious Conflict and the Practice of Toleration in Early Modern Europe* (Cambridge, Mass., 2007).

G. K. Waite, *Heresy, Magic and Witchcraft in Early Modern Europe* (Basingstoke, 2003).

Further reading

Index

Expand your collection of
VERY SHORT INTRODUCTIONS